LITTLE GRAVES

GHOST STORIES
AND SCARY TALES
OF OLD KENTUCKY

To Laurie,
To an old friend who I
share memories with

Harriet A Ruby

HARRIE

Wasteland Press

www.wastelandpress.net
Shelbyville, KY USA

Little Graves:
Ghost Stories and Scary Tales of Old Kentucky
by Harriet A. Ruby

First Printing – February 2022
ISBN: 978-1-68111-455-2

Printed in the U.S.A.

0   1   2   3   4   5   6   7   8

TABLE OF CONTENTS

Introduction

The McCrystal and Henry families migrated to the United States from Ireland in the 1830's. They chose to settle in Mercer County, Kentucky because it reminded them of Ireland.

They were plagued by supernatural occurrences. They relied on religious practices to rid evil spirits from their lives. And closely followed the rules of superstitions to avoid them.

Members of the Ruby family were living in Mercer County by 1793. The Leonard family arrived sixty years later. Though they were religious, they attempted to contact spirits of the dead through seances and other mediums. They were successful in their endeavors many times.

The majority of these stories actually happened to my family members. Others were conveyed to them by friends and neighbors to be true.

These stories have only been offered orally until now. As a child I was frightened by them. As an adult, I embrace them as part of my heritage and Kentucky history.

The appearances of ghost are found in, Around The Bend, The Milk Bottle, Friends Forever, Cave Hill Gentleman, We've Got Company, and several others.

This book takes its title from the story, Little Graves. The story comes from my Grandmother, Claudia Leonard Ruby. As a child she and her brothers participated in an unnatural event, even though they were warned against it. They never expected the outcome to be tragic.

In two stories, In Agreement and Daddy Ruby, spirits of the dead appeared in dreams to family members. One spirit changed a small boy's life forever; the other kept a child from death.

Ghosts haunt the places they knew while they were alive. Many times, they haunt where they died. Unable to move on to the afterlife they became trapped in the living world. Such are the stories, Kitty, Kitty, and Old Man Peters.

Several tales involve pieces of furniture that became possessed. In the story, The Walking Table, evil attaches to an ordinary end table.

Unable to return the table to its normal state, a religious item is put into place. A practice still in use today.

Great Grandma Leonard owned a walnut end table made from the wood of a tree that had been struck by lightning. A bad omen most would say. They used the table to contact the dead. The table tapped its legs back and forth on the floor when communication had been made. On one occasion they called up an evil spirit. The end result wasn't what they had expected.

There are two Mercer County legends in this book. One is Hank The Yankee. He was a Union Civil War soldier that fought in the battle of Perryville, The bloodiest battle in Kentucky. His wasn't the death of a hero.

The other legend, The Unknown Dancer, takes place soon after the end of the Civil War. Questions concerning the unknown dancer haven't ever been answered.

Animals are the focal point in three tales. Trixie Dog, Kitty, Kitty, and The Black Dog. It's been said that cats can see ghost. Kitty, Kitty seems to prove that as a fact.

My Grandmother Henry told me if I encountered a ghost I should ask, "What in God's name do you want?" She said if it was a kindred spirit it would answer my question. If it was an evil spirit the mention of God's name would cause it to leave.

Most of the people involved in these stories are dead now. I wrote this book to share the experiences of another time in Kentucky history.

Hank The Yankee

A Mercer County Legend
1862

Six miles west of Harrodsburg is the small town of Nevada Kentucky. Pronounced Ne-va-de by locals, Nevada is located three miles south-east of The Perryville Battlefield. The bloodiest Civil War battle in Kentucky was fought there in October 1862. Over 1400 men died and 5500 men were wounded.

A Union soldier named Hank and his buddy Jack had decided they had had enough of The Civil War. The pain and suffering were too much for them to bear any longer. Men they marched with lay dead around them. Mangled bodies blown apart by cannonballs hung from tree limbs. A human eye was next to Hank's shoe.

Hank and Jack had managed to stay alive through two years of battle by using their wits. But their time was running out and they knew it.

They planned an escape for a week. They would tell the sentry at the gate they had been instructed to deliver ammunition to the front line. They knew the sentry wouldn't question them and pass them right through.

Hank and Jack would carry an ammunition bag, but there wouldn't be any bullets in it. Instead, it would hold a small amount of food. A blanket would round out the shape of the ammunition bag nicely.

The plan worked perfectly. The sentry didn't question either of them, he barely looked their way. He allowed Hank and Jack to pass through the camps entrance with the wave of his hand.

The two men didn't waste any time putting distance between them and the war. Now was the time for flight.

The central part of Kentucky was in an extreme drought that year. Wells and cisterns had gone dry and the ponds were empty. Water that normally flowed generously from limestone springs were reduced to a trickle. Man and beast had suffered for weeks from lack of water.

The night of their desertion was extremely hot for October. As they ran away from the camp, a thunderstorm in the distant lit the sky with vertical streaks of lightning.

They hurried across a rocky field as it started to rain huge raindrops. The rain pelted their arms hard enough to sting them.

Hank thought of a saying his Grandmother believed to be true. "See big raindrops, soon that rain stops," but it didn't stop. It rained even harder. The sound of thunder vibrated through their bodies.

They came upon a clump of cedar trees and sat down under them. It was the driest place they could find. It was hard for them to tell if the sounds they heard were explosions from cannons or rumbling thunder. The men managed to fall asleep for several hours, and, when they woke up, it was still raining.

Hank cupped his hands together, drinking his fill of rainwater. It was the sweetest water he had tasted in several months. Hank washed his face and hands with the rain and pushed back his hair with his fingers.

"Boy, the rainwater sure tastes good," Hank said to Jack.

"It almost tastes sweet," Jack answered.

The rest and rainwater had given them a second wind. They left the shelter of the cedar trees and walked northeast.

"I hear a river running. Do you hear it?" Hank asked.

"Yes, I hear it."

"It's the Salt River. It runs north. We can follow it out of here. It will take us to the Ohio River and we can cross over into Union territory. We will be safe there. We will travel at night and hide out during the day. That way the Johnny Rebs won't find us."

"Sounds like a good plan to me."

Hank had always hoped if he were to be killed that his death would be fast. Maybe a bullet through his head or his heart. Being critically injured was worse than death. He had seen men whose faces had been blown away from their skulls. The poor souls still alive as they ran around and screamed.

There weren't any doctors or medicine to offer relief from their pain. It was each man for himself. The most you could hope for was a friend would shoot you to put you out of your misery.

Hank and Jack ran faster toward the river. They held their arms out to shield their eyes from cedar branches. Their pace was swift for such a dark night. Hank caught his foot in a wild rose vine. It threw him to ground and twisted his ankle. His body was pricked by the thorns poisonous tips before he could get untangled.

All of a sudden Hank and Jack heard a loud explosion. The noise was so violent that they climbed to the top of a ridge to get a better look. In the distance, they saw massive flames. The sky was orange. It looked like the world was on fire.

"My Lord, look at that Jack."

"What is it?"

"I don't know."

The storm intensified and it started to hail. The men hurried down the hillside to seek refuge. The Salt River was directly in front of them. Hank slipped on the wet riverbank down into the water. The Salt River was running fast and deep from the rain. Hank had to swim back to the rivers bank and Jack pulled him out of the water.

"I've got to rest for a while. I'm exhausted from fighting one battle after another."

"So am I. We can rest up under that bridge for a while."

Both men had dozed off when they were awakened by the sound of horses and men crossing the bridge. From his vantage point, Hank attempted to see what type of uniform the men were wearing. Were they Yankees or Confederates? To his surprise, they appeared to be civilians.

"Hello there, hello there," Hank called out.

Jack stayed hidden under the bridge.

The last rider in the group heard Hank and stopped his horse on the bridge.

"What are you doing Yankee? Are you hiding from someone Yankee?"

"I got lost from my troop during the storm."

"Well, the battle is down this road about two miles, Yankee. That is the direction you should be heading. That is unless you are deserting your troops. Is that what you are doing Yankee? Hey boys, we got ourselves a Yankee deserter here."

The other riders returned to the bridge.

"Well, a Yankee deserter, what should we do with him boys?"

The riders pushed Hank around with the bodies of their horses. One rider had a bullwhip that he struck out in the dark. It hit Hank's cheek, leaving a slash of skin hanging loose. Blood ricocheted in all directions.

"Let's kill this damn Yankee deserter right now. We could hang him by his neck from the bridge railing. He doesn't deserve to live."

Hank begged for his life. "I am not a deserter. I got lost from my unit during this storm. I've waited for the storm to let up under the bridge. I wasn't hiding from anyone. I'm trying to find my way back to Perryville to be with my unit. Please point me in the right direction."

"What do you think Will? What should we do with this Yankee?"

The senior rider said, "Let him go. His fate awaits him down the road."

"Go on Yankee. Follow this road to the first fork, then go to the left. You'll find your kind there."

The riders wheeled their horses around and left Hank standing on the bridge. Hank turned and walked toward the battle, though he had no intentions of going back there. He was just pretending for the rider's sake.

"Thank you, kind sir, for the directions. Thank you for sparing my life."

"Hey Yankee, did you see the big fire in the southwest sky?"

"Yes, I saw it."

"That was the union camp you were looking for, burning up. Some of us good old boys blew you Yankees right out of the state of Kentucky tonight. It was a sight to see. We caught them Yankees totally off guard. I guess they figured we wouldn't attack them during a thunderstorm. Well, they figured wrong. We surrounded them and threw firebombs into that Yankee camp. I saw a damn Yankee on fire. His skin was peeling off his body. I ought to shoot you right where you stand, regardless of what Will said. If you're a deserter, your fate is set. If you're a soldier returning to his unit, your fate is set, so I'm giving you five seconds to get out of my sight, starting now."

Hank ran into the woods and hid under a downed sycamore tree like a frightened rabbit.

After the civilians left, Hank called out to Jack.

"The men are gone Jack. Did you hear what they said?"

"Yeah, I heard them. Do you think it's true?"

"Yes, I think it's true."

Hank and Jack stayed under the bridge for a while. Several hours passed as Hank thought of his buddies he left behind in camp. He thought of the fear they must have felt when they saw the fire ball explode in front of them. Hank imagined how their skin melted away from their bones like wax from a candle. He could see the look on their faces when they realized they were dying.

His thoughts caused him to scream out loud.

"Why did I leave my buddies? Why didn't I stay and fight? How could I be such a coward!"

"We've got to think about ourselves and our families now Hank."

Hank tried to convince himself his decision to desert was due to battle exhaustion. Too much pain and suffering. Too much anger and fear. Dreading the next day made Hank half the man he once was, in stature and in mind.

He ate a piece of hardtack and he drank water from the river. Hank wished he was a dead hero instead of a coward who was alive.

Hank and Jack could smell smoke from a fire. They recognized the smell of human flesh burning. That smell had followed them for two years.

"I can't stand it Jack. It's too late to go back and help our buddies. I don't want to live anymore."

"There isn't anything we can do Hank, except get out of here. What are you doing?"

Hank tore the stripes off the legs of his trousers and tied them together in a double square knot. He tied one end around his neck and the other end around the bridge's rail.

"No, Hank don't do it!"

Hank stepped up on the bridge's railing. Calling out like a crazy person he said,

"God forgive me for being a coward."

Then he jumped, his neck snapped immediately.

Jack was in shock. He returned to his spot under the bridge and cried.

The next morning several Confederate soldiers saw Hanks body hanging from the bridge.

"Look at that damn Yankee coward hanging there," one soldier said to the others.

"Check his pockets for money," another soldier said.

One of the soldiers checked Hanks pockets. The only possession he had was a faded picture of a pretty girl. On the back of the picture it was inscribed, "To Hank."

"He ain't got any money. Just an old picture."

"Cut him down."

"We'll poison the water with his Yankee blood."

"Cut him down now, good enough for a damn Yankee."

A soldier took his knife and sawed the cloth fiber into. Hank fell straight into the river with the noose tied around his neck.

When the Confederate soldiers left, Jack came out from under the bridge. He looked down into the water, but he couldn't see Hank's body.

Jack walked half a mile to the little town of Nevada. Several men stood in front of a store.

"What are you doing here Yankee?" One of the men asked.

"I was wondering if you men could help me retrieve my friend's body from the Salt River. He hung himself off the bridge last night and some Confederates cut him down and his body fell into the river."

"If that damn Yankee killed himself let his body stay in the river. We won't help you. You need to get out of our town. We don't want your type here."

One of the men raised his gun toward Jack.

Jack ran north up the road and didn't look back. There wasn't anything he could do for Hank now.

As the story goes, Hank's spirit never left the bridge. Residents of Mercer and Boyle County consider this area of Mercer County to be haunted by the desperate souls of Civil War soldiers who died during the war.

Many ghostly sightings and unearthly sounds have been heard in Nevada. Especially on Lower Salt River Road near the bridge that spans the river. The bridge where Hank killed himself. Stories have been told of hearing screams of men crying out in pain echoing through the hills. Some said the screams came from wild peacocks that nested on the banks of the river. Others said it wasn't a peacock, it couldn't be. Peacocks don't wail out in agony.

People talked of seeing ghost of Civil War soldiers that appear as dark shadows wandering through the fields at night.

Legend said if you visited Hank's bridge on a full moon his spirit would rise up from the water.

My cousin and I went to Hank's bridge in the 1970's. We had heard the stories and wanted to see for ourselves.

We stood on the bridge and peered over the railing. "You call for Hank. He would be more apt to come for a girl," my cousin said to me.

I was a little afraid but didn't expect anything to happen. So, I started calling out his name.

"Hank, Hank, come up here and see us."

Nothing happened.

"Call out louder. You are not being loud enough."

"Hank, Hank, we are waiting for you. Come on up here!"

To our surprise the water in the river started to spin around. We couldn't look away, we couldn't run away. It was as if our legs wouldn't move.

From deep in the darkness of the water we saw a round white orb the size of a basketball rising up. Closer and closer it rose up toward us. Just before if reached the top of the water, we ran away and didn't look back.

Whether it was the spirit of Hank The Yankee or an illusion I cannot say for sure. But my cousin and I both saw the same thing.

The Unknown Dancer

A Mercer County Legend
1865

Not long after the Civil War ended, the people of Harrodsburg decided to have a fancy ball to celebrate the war being over. The event was held at Graham Springs Hotel, known as the Saratoga Springs of the south. In 1865, the hotel was flourishing with activity in preparation of the big event. Banquet tables were decorated with red, white and blue tablecloths. Wooden folding chairs had ribbons tied around their backs. The chandeliers were draped with paper streamers and cardboard cutouts of stars and flowers. Large crystal punch bowls waited to be filled.

The event was scheduled to begin at 8:00 p.m., but people started arriving by 7:00 p.m. Some walked to the hotel, others came by horse and carriage. Young bachelors wearing stiff necked shirts lined the stone fence that surrounded the hotel. It was an excellent vantage point to watch the pretty girls arrive.

By eight o'clock the ballroom was full of people. The musicians played "My Old Kentucky Home," which brought tears to several eyes.

The ball was in full swing as a Virginia Reel took place on the dance floor. Everyone talked and laughed.

Just as the reel was over, a beautiful woman appeared on the top step. She was breathtaking. Her dark hair swirled around her face in curls. Her black eyes shined like pieces of coal in the sun. She wore a lovely ball gown made of a dark rose satin taffeta material, accented with a flowered silk shawl. The dark eyed woman looked over the crowd, and smiled at everyone who looked her way.

William Fairview, a local bachelor, approached the beautiful stranger.

"Good evening, ma'am, please allow me to welcome you to Harrodsburg. My name is William Fairview."

"Why, thank you kind sir for such a warm welcome."

William extended his arm to her. She placed her right hand upon his arm and he escorted her down the stairs. They were the focus of everyone's attention.

"Would you like to have a seat? My Mother and Aunt have a table on the terrace, there's a nice breeze there, I know they would like to meet you."

"Of course, Mr. Fairview, I would be honored to meet your Mother and Aunt."

The beautiful stranger slipped her arm through Williams and held it tightly.

Surprised by the feel of her touch, he became tense. He wasn't familiar with women who would be so bold as to take a stranger's arm tightly. He wasn't used to it, but he liked it.

"Mother, Aunt Tess, please allow me to introduce you to, I'm sorry Miss, what did you say your name was?"

Right when the girl started to speak, the bugles in the band blew loudly. The horns startled everyone.

"Have a seat my dear," William's Mother told the girl.

The lovely lady sat down. She folded her dress gracefully underneath of herself.

"Are you traveling by yourself Miss?" William's Mother asked.

"Yes, I'm traveling alone."

"Aren't you afraid to travel alone?" Aunt Tess inquired.

"No, there isn't anything to be afraid of."

"I'm not so sure it's the proper thing to do," Aunt Tess added.

"Things have changed since the war ended ma'am."

"May I have this dance Ma'am?" William asked the lovely stranger.

"Certainly."

"William, let the girl rest for a minute, she has just sat down," His Mother said.

"Oh no, I'm fine, I would love to dance."

She extended her hand to William and upon taking it, she squeezed it tightly.

They waltzed around the ball room. William knew every single and married man in the room envied him now. As they danced, William asked her more questions.

"Ma'am, are you from around here?"

"No sir, I am not."

"How did you happen upon this celebration tonight?"

"I was on the train passing through your town, when I heard of this lovely celebration, so I decided to attend. I plan on securing a room here at the hotel for the night, then continuing my journey tomorrow."

"Well, ma'am, I can tell you, I'm sure pleased you decided to join us. Ma'am, what did you say your name was?"

The waltz ended and the applause of the crowd was louder than her answer.

Actually, William wasn't sure she even told him her name. Being the gentleman he was, he didn't ask her again.

"May I escort you back to a seat at the table?"

"Yes, of course."

William sat her at his table and asked, "Would you care for some punch ma'am?"

"Yes, thank you, that would be nice."

"Either of you ladies care for punch?" William asked his Mother and Aunt.

"No, thank you, we're fine for now."

"Are you traveling to meet your parents?" Mrs. Fairview asked her.

"No, I'm afraid not. My parents are dead. They were killed during the war."

"Oh, how terrible!" Aunt Tess exclaimed.

"Do you mind if I ask you how they died?"

"Tess, that is not your business."

"I don't mind to tell you," The lovely stranger answered.

"My Father fought in the war. He was shot in the head less than five miles from where we lived. My Mother died from a broken heart and pneumonia. She stopped eating, took to her bed, and wouldn't get up. The pneumonia sat up in her lungs and three weeks later, she was dead."

"Oh, you poor child, you've had to bear many sufferings for a woman of your age."

"Yes, I have, but my trials and tribulations have made me a stronger person."

"You are very independent. I wish I could have been more independent in my life," Mrs. Fairview commented, "but it wasn't acceptable."

People passed by the table and stared at the beautiful stranger. It seemed impossible to keep your eyes off of her. Her intense beauty, her impeccable clothing and the air of her independence.

"Williams Mother said, "Thank goodness the war is over, people have suffered enough. Did the war cause suffering for you ma'am, besides the death of your parents?"

"The war caused suffering for everyone, no one was spared. Fortunately, I spent the last part of the war in Chicago Illinois. Except for lack of supplies, I faired fairly well."

William returned with her glass of punch and handed it to the stranger. She took the punch cup from his hand, running her finger down his palm in a flirtatious manner. It caused William's face to blush. He looked to see if his Mother or Aunt had noticed, but they hadn't. The beautiful girl sipped her punch slowly.

"If you will excuse me, I believe I will walk around and socialize," She said to William, his Mother and Aunt.

"Of course," They replied.

The beautiful girl floated across the floor with softened steps that appeared not to touch the floor.

Over in the crowd, Martha Simpson talked to her sister, "If Grant himself walked through the front doors now, no one would notice, they would all be looking at that girl. I'm going to go talk to her."

"Hello, my name is Martha Simpson."

"Hello Mrs. Simpson, very nice to meet you," the beauty replied.

"Would you mind me asking where you got such a lovely dress?"

"Not at all Mrs. Simpson. I purchased this gown at Carson, Perry, Scott Department Store in Chicago Illinois."

"You've been to Chicago Miss?"

"Yes, of course, I lived there for a while."

"Oh, how interesting it must be to live in a big city. Have you visited the museums and expositions that are in Chicago?"

"Yes, several times."

Mrs. Simpson continued with her questions. "I suppose you miss Chicago, don't you?"

"I really don't. Chicago was a stopping off place, it wasn't my home."

"Where is your home, Miss?"

Just then, James Peterson stepped in front of the two women. He bowed to the lovely woman and asked, "May I have this dance ma'am?"

"Of course," she said.

James took her hand and lead her to the dance floor. She squeezed his hand tightly.

"My name is James Peterson."

"A pleasure to meet you Mr. Peterson, you are an excellent dancer, and your mighty handsome too, I've always been attracted to dark haired men."

The compliment embarrassed him. He didn't know how to react. He wasn't used to women saying those sort of things. With his head down he replied, "Thank you ma'am."

As soon as one dance was over, another gentleman would ask her to dance. And she obliged. Each man was overcome with her beauty. Their heads swam as they waltzed her around the floor. She flirted with all of them. Smiling, swinging her hair back over her shoulder. She held their hands tightly and looked straight into their eyes.

It was almost midnight and some of the older folks had already gone home. William Fairview meant to have the last dance with the pretty stranger, so he positioned himself at the edge of the dance floor before the next to last song was over. He stepped toward the woman and Billy Sampson.

"May I have the last dance ma'am?"

Billy gave him a hateful look as the stranger stepped over to William.

"This has been such a lovely evening, hasn't it Mr. Fairview?"

"By far the nicest I have spent in a very long while."

"Everyone here has been so nice to me, so friendly, I don't know when I've had a better evening."

"We are pleased you decided to join us ma'am. Harrodsburg is a very friendly town."

"Yes, Mr. Fairview, it seems to be."

The last dance was over and the dancers applauded the evening. William extended his arm to escort her from the dance floor, but she reached for his hand instead.

"Mr. Fairview, I will be taking a room here at the hotel tonight, could you see to those arrangements for me?"

"Of course, ma'am, I'll go right now."

"Thank you, Mr. Fairview, I just need to catch my breathe. I'll join you in the lobby."

William was at the front desk when he heard a commotion in the ballroom. He quickly returned and noticed people were looking at the floor behind the table.

"What's going on?" He asked.

"It's the stranger, she has collapsed to the floor from off of her chair!" Bertha Mayes exclaimed.

"Don't just stand there. Help her up," William insisted.

"I think she has fainted. Her skin is awfully pale," Bertha said.

Mary Tabler fanned the strangers face. Nicholas VanArsdall offered her water, but she couldn't drink.

Several of the men picked the beautiful stranger up off the floor and carried her to a couch in the hotel's lobby. William touched her face in hopes of arousing her, but she didn't move.

"Here's a cold cloth, apply it to her forehead," The hotel manager told William.

William did as he was told but still the stranger showed no improvement.

"Someone get Doctor Traynor right away," William pleaded.

"I'll go get him," James Sampson called out as he rushed out the door.

They elevated the beauty's head and laid the cold washcloth on her forehead. Mary continued to fan her while Bertha patted her hands, but there wasn't any response.

"I don't think she's breathing," Bertha said.

"She has to be."

"Use my compact's mirror, hold it under her nose. If she is breathing the mirror will fog up."

Bertha gave William her compact. He nervously placed the mirror under the strangers nose. She wasn't breathing.

All efforts to revive the beautiful stranger were in vain. When Doctor Traynor arrived he pronounced her dead.

"How could this have happened, she was just waltzing with me?" William explained to the doctor.

"Heart failure took this girls life, no doubt about it."

"I'll have to fill out a death certificate, what was this woman's name?"

"No one knows her name doctor," Bertha said.

"William, weren't you dancing with her? Didn't you ask her name?"

"I did, but wasn't able to hear her answer over the sound of the music. I was embarrassed to ask her again."

"I tried to find out her name when we were dancing, but I didn't," James Sampson said.

"Does anyone know where she came from?"

"She told me she got off the train when she heard about the gala here tonight.

That's all I know," William replied.

"She told Mrs. Simpson she had purchased her gown in Chicago, I do know that," Bertha told everyone.

The doctor announced, "I'll write to the authorities in Chicago and explain the situation. Maybe we will learn of this woman's life, and tell her family members of her death."

"Doctor Traynor, will we bury her body here in Harrodsburg?" William asked.

"There aren't any other options."

The next day a memorial service was held for the beautiful unknown dancer. Burial was on the grounds of Graham Springs, on the top of a knoll. This location later became Young's Park. A sign was erected that read.

Hallowed and hushed be the place of the dead.
Step softly, bow head
The grave of the unknown dancer

The Harrodsburg Hospital overlooks Young's park. For many years, nurses, patients and visitors have seen a woman dancing across the grounds of the park on moonlit nights. Two of my Aunts saw her.

Their description of the woman is always the same. She's wearing a long flowing formal dress. Waving a long scarf behind her as she appears to be dancing on air.

The woman has approached several people over the years. She always says the same thing, "I can't find my way home." Then she disappears.

You can visit the grave of the unknown dancer today. Perhaps if you go on a moonlit night, you will see her too.

In A Window's Reflection

1880

L ife was hard for Mrs. Bessie Lewis. Her husband was killed in a farming accident when he slipped and fell into the blades of a wheat trashing machine on Mr. Silas Huff's farm. His casket was nailed closed during the funeral because there wasn't much of him left to bury after they picked him out of the thrasher blades.

The Lewis' little farm was six miles west of Harrodsburg. There was a four room house, an outhouse, and a barn that leaned to the east, sitting on twelve acres. For each shovel of dirt on the farm, there was a half a shovel of rocks. Upon her husband's death, the farm became her's and her seven children's. They tended the farm the best they could.

Mrs. Lewis had seven children. John was the oldest, followed by Jean, James, Joshua, Joseph, June and Jacob. Mrs. Lewis and her older daughters were good seamstresses. They sewed for many people in the county. The older boys took any odd jobs they could find and between all of their work they managed to survive.

Mr. Lewis had dug a deep root cellar two years earlier. The last project he completed before he was killed. It had proven to be an excellent root cellar for preserving and storing their food. Knowing her husband had sit the rocks in place for the cellar soothed her. Mrs. Lewis would touch the rock walls, sensing his touch.

Sunday was the Lord's day and The Lewis' respected it. When they returned to their farm after church they relaxed and enjoyed each other's company.

Jacob tended to stay close to his Mama most of the time. Being the baby had kept Jacob rather shy. Mrs. Lewis hoped Jacob would overcome his shyness. He needed to be stronger in mind to survive the life that lay ahead of him.

Out on the front porch, Jean was singing a song, trying to get Jacob to dance with her. He finally agreed and they had danced around and around on the front porch. But as soon as the dance was over, Jacob returned to his Mama's side.

"You know what would be a fun thing to do?" Mrs. Lewis asked her children.

"What, Mama, what?"

"Let's rake up the sugar maple leaves. We don't want to leave them on the ground all winter since they would kill the grass. After they are raked you can jump in the pile and play in the leaves. It will be fun."

They racked the leaves into a big pile. Using their hands and arms to scoop the leaves into a huge pile. Mrs. Lewis handed John a garden rack, and the house broom to Jane.

The children ran and jumped into the leaf pile. They threw the leaves up into the air. The crisp wind of fall blew the leaves into a swirl that resembled a cyclone.

James climbed up the maple tree. He grabbed his rope, and swung himself down to the ground.

Jacob covered himself in the leaves, then crawled through them like they were a tunnel. Everybody was laughing and enjoying themselves.

"It's getting late. Better come on in the house and wash up. We've got to get supper ready."

"Yes, Mama."

At the supper table they talked and laughed about their day.

Mrs. Lewis told the children. "Tomorrow we will have a bond fire and burn the pile of leaves. Then we will put the ashes on the garden. It will be good for the soil."

"That will be fun Mama."

Mrs. Lewis took off her apron and sat down in her rocking chair. Jacob walked over and leaned his head on her shoulder. She put her arm around him and patted his back.

All of a sudden Jacob screamed out.

"Mama, Mama, look at that. There is a little colored girl looking through the window at us. She's crying."

"What? Where is she?"

"She's right there at the window."

Mrs. Lewis looked toward the window and saw what looked like a puff of smoke rising up into the air. She ran over to the window for a better look but there wasn't anything there.

"What did she look like Jacob?"

She looked like June, except she was black. She was the same size as June, and was wearing a dress like the one that June wears to church. She had her hands cupped around her face so she could see in here. I looked at her straight in her eyes. She was crying. Then all of a sudden she was gone."

The other children ran into the kitchen to see what was happening.

"What's he talking about Mama?" John asked.

"Your brother saw someone at the window."

"Who was it Mama?" Jane asked.

"I'm not sure. I thought I saw a puff of smoke, but it probably was a shadow. You boys go outside and look around."

The boys took a kerosene lantern with them to look around for the little colored girl. But there wasn't anyone there.

"You must have been dozing off to sleep when you saw the aberration," his sister Jane said to Jacob.

"I swear that I saw a little colored girl looking in the window," Jacob said with conviction, You believe me don't you Mama?"

"I believe that you saw something at the window. There doesn't seem to be anyone on our property now. Whoever it was must have run away. Let's all get to bed. We'll have a big day tomorrow."

As soon as the morning chores were done, the children were anxious to burn the leaf pile.

"Can we burn the leaf pile now Mama?"

Mrs. Lewis stepped out on the front porch. She commented on how the wind seemed to be picking up. She told her son John to fetch a bucket of water, just in case the fire got out of control. John obeyed his Mother and quickly returned with the water. James used a kitchen match to start the fire.

Mrs. Lewis could hear her children talk as the dry leaves popped. She couldn't smell the leaves burning as the wind blew the smoke away from the house, taking the aroma with it.

She sat down at the kitchen table and began breaking a late crop of green beans, they would have for supper.

All of a sudden, the curtains sucked out the kitchen window from the wind changing direction. Mrs. Lewis could smell the leaves burning now.

Suddenly from the front yard, screams erupted. Mrs. Lewis ran through the front door out into the yard and saw John running for the bucket of water. Jane and Joseph were screaming. James and Joshua ran toward their Mama with a terrified look in their eyes. There was so much going on that Mrs. Lewis couldn't realize what was happening.

John grabbed the bucket of water and threw it on a burning mass on the ground. All of the children screamed again. Mrs. Lewis ran toward John, realizing at that time her daughter June was on fire.

The little girl had stopped screaming now. Her lifeless burned body didn't move. The other children stood on the porch struck with fear. John had managed to put the fire out that had enveloped his sister, but all efforts were too late. June was dead.

"Run to the house and bring a blanket here," Mrs. Lewis told her son, "The rest of you children stay on the porch and don't move."

John returned with the blanket, and covered Junes charred body with it.

"What happened John?"

"All of a sudden the wind changed directions Mama. June's apron blew away from her body and caught on fire. It all happened so fast we were caught off guard."

The children, stood on the front porch and cried. Jane was holding Jacob and Joshua. James was kneeling down with his head in his hands. Joseph stood with his back turned away from the situation.

"All of you children go into the house and stay there until I call for you."

"Yes, Mama,"

Mrs. Lewis told John to go to the neighbor's house and tell them what had happened to June. Neighbors always helped each other, especially when a tragedy occurred. Mrs. Lewis would need help with June's body.

"Jean, Jean," Mrs. Lewis called out.

"Stop the clock and cover the mirrors."

These practices were common at the death of a family member. Clocks were stopped to verify time of death and mirrors were covered with sheets to prevent the image of the dead from appearing in them. It was thought that if the image of the dead appeared in the mirror, the dearly departed's soul and spirit would be captured in the mirror, and couldn't go on to heaven.

Within twenty minutes, Mrs. Lewis heard voices coming down the lane toward her house. Mr. and Mrs. Wiley were the first to come into her sight. Then her son John returned with Mr. Graham and his son, George.

Mr. Wiley helped Mrs. Lewis up off the ground and told her to go into the house with his wife.

"We'll see to June for you," Mr. Wiley said.

Mrs. Wiley helped Mrs. Lewis into the house. As soon as they walked in the children ran to their Mama.

"Is June dead?" Jane asked.

"Yes, she is."

The children started to cry again. The thought of their sister being dead was too much for them to handle. They still hadn't recovered from the death of their father, and now their sister was dead too.

The men wrapped June up in the blanket and brought her body into the house. They took the corpse into the bedroom and laid the dead child's body on the bed.

Mrs. Wiley told John and George Graham to go and get Mrs. Carey and her sister, Mrs. Terhune. Women would be needed to prepare the body for burial. He returned with them immediately.

Mr. Wiley and Mr. Graham asked. "Mrs. Lewis, is there any lumber on the farm that we could use to build a coffin? We won't need much."

"There's lumber in the barn. James, show the men where the lumber is. There's nails in a coffee can on the shelf out there too."

"Yes, ma'am."

"We'll need to straighten June's body up, for the viewing," Mrs. Wiley told Mrs. Lewis.

She got up from her chair and filled up a washpan with water. She lay a bar of lye soap and clean wash cloth beside the wash pan.

Mrs. Carey and Mrs. Terhune carried the wash pan and soap toward the bedroom where poor June laid covered up with the blanket. Mrs. Wiley got the towel, wash rag and hair comb. They told Mrs. Lewis, "Go on into the kitchen with the children."

But Mrs. Lewis insisted she would help prepare her youngest daughter's body for burial.

When Mrs. Carey removed the blanket from June's body, she gasped at the sight. The poor little things body was burnt black. Even her hair was burnt to the roots on her head.

Mrs. Carey sponged off June's body but there really wasn't much she could do. The burned skin peeled away. Mrs. Terhune tried to smooth her hair down, but it was as course as steel wool. The comb wouldn't pass through it.

Mrs. Lewis brought the little blue dress that June wore to church into the bedroom. Now, June's Sunday dress would be used for her funeral shroud.

The men returned from the barn with the primitive coffin that they had built. Mrs. Lewis used her best winter blanket to line it.

The men said. "Mrs. Lewis, we'll go on up to the cemetery and dig a grave for June."

"Bury her next to her dear Daddy."

By three o'clock that afternoon over twenty people arrived to view the body and console the family. People brought plates of food to the wake. The women fixed plates for everyone who came into the house. Most of the men stood outside drinking moonshine or strong coffee.

June's coffin was situated on a pair of wooden sawhorses, sitting against the far wall of the kitchen.

Everyone gathered around. Some cried, others prayed.

Mrs. Simms asked Mrs. Lewis. "How can you stand to bury your youngest daughter?"

"I have to stand it for my other children. That's all there is to it."

It was a sensible answer.

Mrs. Lewis straightened out June's dress and motioned for her children to come closer. John, Joseph and James were the first to reach the coffin. Upon seeing their little sister, they hid their faces and cried. The three boys ran out the front door of the house and ran away to be by themselves.

Jane held Joshua's hand as they walked toward the coffin. They cried, in fear of seeing June's dead body.

Mrs. Lewis motioned for Jacob to approach the coffin. Barely moving, he slowly made his way across the room as he stared down at the floor. Jacob hadn't ever seen a dead body before. He was too young to remember his Daddy's funeral. When he finally looked into the casket, he grasped for breath and said,

"Mama, Mama that's not June's body in the coffin. That's the body of that little colored girl I saw looking through the window at us last night!"

Mrs. Lewis felt a chill run down her neck. She hugged her son tightly.

Mrs. Carter overheard what Jacob had said to his Mother so she asked Mrs. Lewis a question.

"Did Jacob foretell of June's death?"

"Jacob saw a little black girl looking through the window at us last night. He said she was crying and had on a dress that was like the one June wore to church. I suppose it is possible that he saw June's burned dead body in a premonition. I had never taken into consideration he was the seventh child of a seventh son, but his Daddy was the seventh son in his family. I just never had thought about it."

"It's a curse, not a gift, you realize that don't you Mrs. Lewis?"

"Yes, I'm afraid I do."

Time To Go

1880

Poor old Grandpa Henry had suffered for years from heart problems and crippling arthritis. His fingers curled into his hands and he began forgetting everything. He would try to put two shoes on the same foot and his shirt on backwards. Doctor Sullivan said Grandpa had hardening of the arteries. What we know today as Alzheimer's disease.

Grandpa's children took turns seeing to his needs. One of his children had been at the homeplace every day since Grandma Henry died five years earlier.

Some days Grandpa was sensible, while other days he talked of stories that had happened fifty years ago. He would ask for Grandma or his old dog, Blue. The children didn't argue with him or tell him those days were over. They were kind and respectful.

One night Grandpa told his daughter Sarah, "When the death wagon comes, I'm ready to go."

"There's not any death wagon coming here, Papa, I assure you."

"No, it's coming. It will be here any day."

"What makes you think that?"

"I just know," he replied.

The next day, Sarah mentioned to her sister, Mattie, "Last night Papa said the death wagon was coming to get him."

"What is a death wagon?" Mattie asked.

I'm not sure what it is. I guess it's a ghost wagon, or maybe it's some type of funeral hearse."

"I've never heard of one."

When their brother William came Sara asked, "William, have you ever heard of a death wagon?"

"No, I can't say that I have. What are you talking about?"

"Last night Papa said the death wagon was coming."

"Was that before or after he drank his tonic?" William grinned.

"Before he drank it," Sarah smiled.

William said, "I'm going over to St. Nicholas church this afternoon, I'll ask Father Voit about it. Maybe he will know what a death wagon is."

"Let us know what he says."

"I will."

The girls got Grandpa out of bed and sat him up in his chair to bathe him.

"That water is cold as ice," Grandpa protested. "Are you trying to kill me?"

"No, Papa, the water is nice and warm."

"Is the death wagon here yet?"

"No, Papa, there isn't any death wagon."

"Yes, there is. It will be coming for me."

"Papa, what is a death wagon?" Mattie asked.

"Don't you have any sense, girl? You never heard of a death wagon?"

"No, Papa, I haven't."

"The death wagon came when your Mama died. I saw it. I saw your Mama's soul climb into it."

"Papa, you must have had a bad dream."

"Damn it, girl, I know what I'm talking about."

Grandpa fretted and wrestled with his daughters.

"Papa, calm down." Mattie said in a soothing voice. "If you say there is a death wagon, we believe you."

"Well, you will see, when the wagon comes for me."

They dressed Grandpa and helped him to his favorite chair. Several times that morning he called to his daughters, "Who's that driving up the road?"

Looking out they didn't see anyone.

"There isn't anyone out there Papa."

"I heard a wagon coming up the road. Go find out who it was."

"Papa, there's no one here."

"I heard a wagon coming down the lane. It had to come here."

"Maybe it turned around and left before we saw it," Sarah said.

"Maybe it did," Grandpa said as he relaxed.

Before dinner, Mattie heard horses neighing. She figured it was William coming home to eat so she waited, but he never came in. Mattie looked out the back door toward the barn lot. Everything was quiet.

"I swore I heard horses neighing," she told her sister.

"It's probably William."

"No, it wasn't William. There wasn't anybody outside."

They let the thought go as they cooked supper.

Soon afterwards William returned.

"Who's been here?" he asked.

"No one has been here. Why do you ask?"

"There are fresh wagon tracks on the lane."

"I thought I heard horses, but when I looked, I didn't see anything," Mattie told her brother.

They ate supper at the kitchen table, while Grandpa napped in another room. Sarah would feed him when he woke up.

"William, did you ask Father Voit about the death wagon?"

"Oh, yeah, I did. He said it was an old Irish superstition. Sort of a way for your soul to catch a ride to heaven. The death wagon is a good thing, not bad, according to Father Voit. He said it is a covered wagon with a black canvas top that is pulled by a pair of black Belgium Draft Horses, but there doesn't seem to be a driver. The wagon will appear right before someone dies, then disappear into a white fog. If you see the wagon and horses, you will be the next one to die. Father said he had never heard of anyone who had actually seen the death wagon."

Mattie interrupted her brother. "Papa said he saw it when Mama died. He said he saw her spirit climb into the back of the wagon. Then it disappeared into a cloud of fog."

"It is time to go! It is time to go!" Grandpa yelled from the other room. His children ran to see what was the matter.

"Papa, what is it?"

"It's time to go. The death wagon is heading down the lane."

"Papa, you've had another bad dream."

"It's time to go," his anxiousness frightened them.

"Calm down, Papa, calm down."

"Look at that?" William said, pointing to Grandpa's hands. For the first time in fifteen years the children watched in amazement as his fingers straightened out. Grandpa sighed a heavy sigh and died.

"Oh, no," The girls started to cry.

William covered Grandpa's body with a blanket.

Through her tears Sarah said, "I hear someone coming."

"It's probably Father Voit. He said he might stop by."

"I hope it is. He can bless Papa's body and soul," Mattie cried.

They all heard the neigh of horses and the sound of wagon wheels as they bumped over the rocky lane. Father's Voit's buggy was lightweight and he only used one horse, so it wasn't him arriving.

"Oh, my Lord," Sarah cried.

Mattie and William looked at her. A white mist rose from Grandpa's body. It passed directly between William and Mattie and swirled clockwise out the window.

They stood motionless, wanting to move but afraid to.

"Should we look out the window?" William asked his sisters.

"No, don't look. You could be the next to die," his sisters pleaded.

"I've got to look. I may never have another chance to see the death wagon, if that is what it is."

Mattie and Sarah covered their eyes.

William heard the horse's neigh. When he looked out the window he thought he saw a large object, but it was hard to tell. There was too much dust stirred up. As if a wagon had just passed by.

The Empty Milk Bottle

1881

Elmer Thompson operated a grocery store down at Duncan Kentucky. A two-room log cabin with wood floors and dark shelving. Mr. Thompson carried a variety of items, from pillow ticking to fine Kentucky tobacco. His store was a meeting place for the entire community. If there was news to be heard, Mr. Thompson's store was the place to hear it. Folks gathered on the porch to talk on warm days and when the weather got cold, they moved inside the store. Mr. Thompson kept a fire burning in a cast iron stove that always had a pot of strong black coffee simmering on it. Sometimes it was hard to shop for what you needed there were so many people in the store.

Early one morning while straightening his yard goods, Mr. Thompson realized he wasn't alone. He turned around to see a thin woman wearing a flowered dress standing in front of him.

"Poor thing," he thought to himself.

"Sorry Miss, I didn't hear you come in, what can I do for you?"

"Milk bottle," she said.

"Oh, you want to buy a milk bottle?"

She nodded her head yes, but said nothing.

He reached under the shelf and sat the milk bottle on the counter.

"Milk."

"You want milk too?"

"Yes."

Mr. Thompson took the empty bottle over to the milk can and filled it up.

"That will be three cents."

The woman reached for the milk bottle but said nothing. Mr. Thompson noticed her hands and arms were skin and bones. Her complexion looked almost transparent, and her eyes were a washed out blue.

The dress she wore appeared to be store bought and brand new. Elmer wondered how a woman who looked so bad physically could afford a new dress. He watched her turn around and walk out of his store with the bottle of milk.

Elmer thought to himself that the woman looked familiar, but he couldn't think who she was. Even though he knew everybody who lived around that part of the county.

"She's so pitiful," he thought. "She must really need the milk badly, her children must be starving."

Mr. Thompson continued to straighten the shelves and soon his mind left the thought of the pitiful woman.

The next day, around the same time, the woman appeared again. She was wearing the same flowered print dress as she was wearing yesterday. But today the dress had dried dirt on it. Her hair seemed to be pasted to her head.

"Well, how are you today?" Elmer asked her.

She said nothing as she sat the empty milk bottle on the counter.

"Were you wanting to get more milk today?"

She didn't answer. She just scooted the milk bottle his way.

Elmer filled the bottle with milk, and wiped the drips from the sides on his apron. He sat it down in front of her.

"That will be three cents Miss. By the way, you look familiar to me. Do I know you? Are you staying around here with kin folk?

The woman didn't answer him. She took the milk and walked out the door.

Mr. Thompson thought to himself, "I can't keep giving my milk away for free. If she comes in tomorrow, I'll offer her a job here at the store. She could help me clean and restock the shelves. Yep, that's what I'll do, the poor woman needs help."

The next day he waited for her to arrive. Again, he was startled by her presence as he turned around. The woman stood there with the same empty milk bottle in her hand. She wore the same dress, and the color of her skin had faded to a deathly white. Her eyes looked invisible.

"Oh, hello, how are you this morning?"

She didn't answer him. She just sat the empty milk bottle on the counter.

Mr. Thompson began talking to her. "I was planning on hiring some help around here. Business has been good lately. I'm thinking of adding on a small kitchen in the back. I was wondering if you would be interested in the job?"

She didn't reply. Her thin hand pushed the milk bottle toward him.

He filled the milk bottle again and watched as the woman took it and left the store.

This time he decided to follow her to see where she was going. She walked down past Mrs. Lettie Smith's house, crossed the road and walked into the yard of The Salvation Baptist Church. Elmer noticed she struggled to take her next step.

"The poor thing is so weak she can barely walk," he thought to himself.

Elmer watched her walk to the side of the church and she disappeared over the hill. He hurried to catch up with her and when he reached the rise of the hill he couldn't believe what he saw. The woman walked to a fresh dug grave, stood over it, and disappeared down into the earth.

"I must be seeing things," he said out loud.

He shook his head several times, and rubbed his eyes. He drew in a good breath and went over to the grave site. He examined the name on the wooden cross. It read, Kathleen Addams and son, William. It was the grave of Francis Utterly's daughter and grandson.

They had been killed four days earlier in a terrible buggy accident. The harness had broken and the buggy went out of control. It rolled to the bottom of the hill and slammed into a tree.

The woman and her child had been buried together in the same grave. A common practice at the time.

Mr. Thompson felt of his forehead and thought he must be sick with the fever. What he had seen couldn't have happened. Just when he started to leave the grave site, he heard a baby cry. He listened intently. It sounded as if the crying was coming from the grave.

Elmer left the cemetery and returned to his store. Several people had gathered out front waiting for him to return. One of them happened to be Sheriff Price.

"Sheriff Price, you know I'm not a drinking man, don't you?" Elmer asked.

"I've never seen you drunk Elmer. Why in the world are you asking me that?"

"All of you are going to think I'm crazy, but for the last three days a sickly-looking woman wearing a flowered print dress came into my store wanting milk in a baby bottle. I've filled it up for her every time, but she never paid me for it. In fact, she never said hardly anything to me."

"So today I decided to follow her to see where she went. She walked down the road to the church's cemetery and disappeared over the hill. When I reached the top of the hill, I saw the woman step down on a fresh dug grave and she disappeared into the ground. I couldn't believe my eyes! I slowly walked to the grave site and read the name on the wooden cross. It was the grave of Francis Utterly's daughter, Kathleen Addams, and her son William."

The men shook their heads in disbelief.

One of the men commented, "Elmer, you must have eaten a bad piece of meat this morning and it's made you sick, you better go sit down."

"I'm not sick, and I don't need to sit down, I know what I saw. The thing is, I haven't told you the whole story yet. When I walked away from the grave, I heard a baby crying."

"Where was the baby at?" Sheriff Price asked him.

"It sounded like the crying was coming from the grave."

"Oh Elmer, you are making this story up as you go along," Ned Chestnut yelled out.

"No, I'm not!"

"Well, it's a mighty strange story. I think we should go up to the cemetery and see what is going on up there," the sheriff told the men.

They all agreed to go to the cemetery with him.

"Elmer, you better bring your shovel with you, just in case," the sheriff said.

"In case of what?" Ned Chestnut asked.

"In case we need it," Sheriff Price said.

When the men got to the grave there was nothing but silence. Not a bird singing or a cricket chirping. It was almost an eerie silence. The men looked at each other.

"What do we do now?" Elmer asked the sheriff.

"The dirt looks awfully loose to have been down here for four days. You would have thought it would have settled more by now. It almost looks like it's been dug back out. I say we leave it this way, and go back to your store. I could use a cup of coffee."

The men turned to leave. They hadn't taken three steps away from the grave when they heard a noise. It was the sound of a baby crying.

"Did you hear that?" Ned asked the men.

"Of course, we heard it Ned, we definitely heard it."

"I swear it sounds like it's coming from the grave, give me your shovel Elmer."

The sheriff started to dig the dirt out of the grave. The more dirt he dug, the louder the crying became.

"Come over here and give me a hand boys."

Elmer, Nicholas and Ned did what the Sheriff asked. They dug the dirt out of the grave with their hands. Elmer used a piece of oak bark to scoop the loose dirt away.

All of a sudden, the Sheriff's shovel hit something. It was the wooden coffin. Elmer and Nicholas got down into the grave and heaved the casket up to the Sheriff and Ned.

Between the slates on the top of the coffin they saw movement. Sheriff Price pried open the coffin. There in the coffin was Francis Utterly's daughter's body. She was wearing the flowered dress she had worn to Elmer's store. In her arms, her son squinted his eyes at the daylight, and started to cry. Beside the baby there was an empty milk bottle.

"Is this the woman you saw at your store?" Sheriff Price asked Elmer.

"Yes, it is."

"Didn't you recognize her?"

"No, I hadn't seen her for two years. Not since she married Bernard Addams and moved to Lebanon."

The Sheriff wrapped the baby in his jacket and the men returned to Mr. Thompson's store. Ned was sent to get the baby's family.

"How could this have happened?" Elmer asked Sheriff Price.

The Sheriff wiped the sweat from his brow and said, "That buggy went over the cliff down on Hilltop Road. It was completely destroyed when it hit the tree. The woman suffered massive injuries to her body and the baby didn't have a heartbeat, so we figured he was dead too. We buried them the same afternoon of the wreck. It's a strange thing."

"It sure is," Elmer said, "I tell you what Sheriff Price, I can say I've seen a ghost now. I never had before, and don't care if I ever do again."

But Elmer, you are the hero. You saved the baby by giving its ghostly mother the milk that it needed to survive. You discovered the baby's cry. You are the hero Elmer."

Everyone at the store agreed. They all patted Elmer on the back and shook his hand.

The news spread fast around Duncan. Especially news about such a thing as a dead woman who saved her baby from starving. Her spirit left the cold and damp grave and walked among the living.

Less than thirty minutes after the baby was found, the Utterly's came to fetch him. The baby's father fell to his knees, and thanked God. He proclaimed it a miracle that his son had been found alive.

The Knapping Hammer

1882

Papa McCrystal had a stroke when he was in his eighties. He spent most of his time in bed and his family took care of him. Sometimes when he talked, he made perfect sense, sometimes he didn't.

One night when his son was visiting, Papa McCrystal asked for his knapping hammer. The one he had used for years to break rocks for stone fences and roads.

His family tried to calm him down, but he insisted he wanted his hammer.

"Don't give him the hammer. He might hurt himself," Mom said.

"I want my knapping hammer now. I have to take it with me when I go."

"You're not going anywhere tonight. You need to settle down," his son John told him.

After a while Papa calmed down and the family went into the kitchen. They were sitting around the table talking when, all of a sudden, a loud noise echoed through the house.

Bam, Bam, Bam.

"What in the world is that?" Mom asked.

"I don't know," John answered.

Bam, Bam, Bam.

"It sounds like it's coming from the chimney."

"I bet it is an old raccoon up there stirring around."

Bam, Bam, Bam.

"That's not an old coon."

"How do you know that?"

"Because raccoons don't pound in the count of threes."

"No, I guess they don't. What is it then?"

Bam, Bam, Bam.

Just then Papa cried out from his bedroom.

"I want my hammer now! Get it for me. Please!"

"Mom, please give the poor old man his hammer. He wants it."

Bam, Bam, Bam.

Bam, Bam, Bam.

"I don't know where the hammer is. It might be in the shed, or the barn. I don't know where it is."

Bam, Bam, Bam.

"I'll look for the hammer and then I'll find out where the noise is coming from," John assured her.

John went to the barn. Mom remained at the table and listened to the sounds coming from the chimney.

Papa cried out louder than before. "Please bring me my knapping hammer. I have to take it with me."

Bam, Bam, Bam.

Suddenly Mom realized that it was an omen of death. Knocking sounds on the walls of the house always meant a death was near.

Bam, Bam, Bam.

John returned from the barn. "I can't find the hammer. It isn't in the barn or the shed. Where else could it be?"

"You know what the hammer looks like, don't you? It has a round head and it's on a hickory handle."

"I know what his knapping hammer looks like, Mom."

Bam, Bam, Bam.

Papa screamed in pain. Mom and John ran to his bedside.

"What is it Papa? What is wrong?"

Papa gasped in a weakly voice. "I want my knapping hammer."

He took one more breath and died.

They pulled the bedcovers over his face to cover the expression of pain and misery on his face.

John and Mom returned to the kitchen.

Bam, Bam, Bam.

Bam, Bam, Bam.

"While you were outside, I realized what the noise is."

"What is it Mom?"

"It was an omen of death. And now your father is dead."

"I wish I could have found Papa's hammer before he died. He wanted it so badly."

"I don't know where it could be."

Bam, Bam, Bam.

All of a sudden, the fire in the fireplace flared up. They looked to see what had happened.

"There is something in the fire. I can't tell what it is. I'll get the tongs and get it out."

Mom stood back while John pulled the object from the flames, it was flaming red hot. John dropped it on the floor.

They both looked down in astonishment. There was Papa's knapping hammer, its round iron head burned red and the hickory handle was charred.

"How is that possible?" Mom asked.

"Mom, I remember now. A couple of years ago Papa and I were working on the chimney when he dropped the hammer down the flue. I had forgotten all about it."

"Mom, how did the hammer happen to show up tonight of all nights?"

"Papa was willing it to fall down so he could have it when he died. I told you the noise was an omen."

"John wipe off the hammer and take it to Papa. Lay it beside his body. It's a shame we didn't find it before he died."

"All right, Mom."

John took the knapping hammer to Papa's bedroom and laid it beside his body.

Mom and John talked and made plans for Papa's funeral.

"We will bury him tomorrow after we tell the family. Tonight, we need to wash his body and have it prepared for the funeral."

"Yes, Mom, I'll get a pan of water and soap. You get his comb and clothes."

They both walked into the bedroom.

"Oh, you put his hand on the knapping hammer. That was nice."

"I didn't put Papa's hand on the hammer. I just laid it beside him."

"Well, he's holding the handle now!"

They lifted the covers from Papa's face. The pain and misery they had seen on his face earlier was gone. Papa now looked happy and serene.

Daddy Ruby

Circa 1890

All of us dream. Some remember our dreams, some of us don't. In the case of my Grandfather Ruby, his whole life was drastically changed because of a dream.

My Grandfather, Uniford Bury Ruby, was born November 29th, 1887 to Levi and Alice Wright Ruby of Mercer County. When he was two years old his family moved to Anadarko Oklahoma.

Work was hard to find in Kentucky at that time and Alice's sister Margaret and her husband, Grayson Bottoms offered Levi a job in Anadarko. Grayson and Margaret had moved to Oklahoma to start a school to teach Cherokee Indians farming techniques.

So, the decision was made that Levi, Alice, Uniford and Viola, Alice's daughter from her first marriage, would move out there. They packed up what few possessions they owned into their wagon and headed southwest.

The trip produced one problem after another. Recent rains washed out the roads and many trees were down. Driving the wagon through such rough terrain caused two spokes on a wheel to break. It took a day to repair them. After forty-seven days they arrived in Anadarko.

Alice was thrilled to be with her sister Maggie. They all lived together in a large canvas tent. The Indians on the reservations lived in teepees.

Alice was fascinated by the strength of the Cherokee women's spirits and how they were able to survive without nothing.

The Indians were willing to learn all they could from Grayson and Levi. They introduced new crops to the Indians, such as beets and sweet potatoes. They showed them how to plow the ground by using their horses, then, fertilize the same field with the horse's waste.

This period of time included the land rush of 1889-1891. The government was offering land taken from the Indians to people who would move into the area and stake a claim. Hundreds of people came to the Oklahoma territory to stake a claim. The town of Anadarko turned into a mad house.

With very little rhyme or reason, the claims were handed out on a certain day.

People stood at the edge of town, when without warning, a loud siren would blow. In a mass exodus the people ran toward the countryside to choose a plot of land. People who were better prepared had already chosen sights and immediately placed stakes in the ground to claim the property. The other people were forced to go farther away from town to claim their ground.

Several months passed and the Ruby family had settled into a routine. One day Alice announced she was going to have a baby. Everyone was very happy about it. In no time at all she gave birth to a daughter that she named Maggie.

Maggie was sickly from the start. She didn't gain weight even though she was eating well. The Indian women made poultices from herbs for the child. They brought goat's milk for her to drink because it is very high in iron. The baby girl drank it, but it didn't help her. Within four months of her birth, Maggie was dead.

Maggie was buried on the reservation on a rainy Sunday afternoon. Alice refused to leave the graveside and eventually Levi had to carry her home.

Alice never recovered from the loss of her baby girl. She took to her bed and stayed there. She cried day and night. She refused to eat, drink or talk to anyone.

Heartbroken over the death of his daughter, and worrying that his wife was dying, Levi began to lose focus. It seemed in some ways, he wished Alice would go on and die. He wanted to take Uniford and Viola back to Kentucky. There wasn't any way Alice would survive the trip. She was too frail and fragile to leave her bed.

It was said that Levi, not in his right mind, threw cold water under Alice's bed to make her sicker, so that she would go on and die.

In less than a month, Alice worried, fretted and starved herself to death. They buried her in a grave right beside of little Maggie. They covered the graves with stone boulders to keep the coyotes from digging her up.

Levi mourned for his wife and daughter. He found it difficult to concentrate on his work on the reservation. He would forget what task he was doing and start to cry.

Margaret and Grayson convinced Levi to take Uniford and Viola back to Kentucky. They knew Levi wouldn't survive the trip in a wagon, being as downhearted as he was.

Margaret wrote a letter to her father, Charles Wright in Kentucky. Telling him about the unfortunate situation they were in.

When he read the letter, he took a purse full of money, climbed on a train and left Kentucky for Anadarko.

Charles brought Levi, Uniford and Viola back to Kentucky on the train. Levi and Uniford moved in with Levi's father, Jim Ruby. Viola went to live with her aunt in Washington County.

Levi became weaker every day. In less than three weeks of returning to Kentucky, Levi died from consumption. Uniford was three years old when his Daddy died.

Jim Ruby was an old man by that time and he couldn't take care of Uniford, so other arrangements had to be made.

Jim sent Uniford to live with the Warner family down in Washington County too. Mary Warner had been Jim Ruby's second wife, so she was Uniford's step grandmother.

Another of Alice's sister's, Francis Wright Horn lived in Mercer County. She worried about Uniford living with his Grandfather down at Battle, Kentucky. But having twelve children of her own, she was kept too busy to think about Uniford every day. At the time, Francis didn't know Uniford had been taken to the Warner's farm in Washington County.

One night, Francis had a dream about her sister Alice. Alice came to her, begging Francis to go and get Uniford and bring him back to Mercer County. Alice told Francis in the dream that Uniford was in Washington County with Mary Warner and that the Warner's treated the little boy badly.

The dream was very vivid to Francis and the next day she made several inquiries about where Uniford was living. She soon discovered he was living with the Warner's in Washington County, so she made immediate plans to go and get the boy.

Her hired hand, Dalton League, drove her in a buggy to Washington County that afternoon. When they arrived at the Warner's place, Francis saw Uniford carrying wood into the house. She called out his name, but he didn't know her and went on into the house. Francis knocked on the front door. Mary Warner opened the door.

"What can I do for you today, Mrs. Horn?"

"I've come to take Uniford home with me. He should be raised with his own family. It wasn't your place to take him in, but you did. I appreciate it, Mary."

"How did you know Uniford was here?"

"I knew because the spirit of my dead sister Alice, Uniford's Mother, came to me in a dream. She told me where he was and who he was with. She begged me to come and get him, and so I have. Can we get Uniford's things together so that we can get back to Harrodsburg before dark?"

"Are you telling me his Mother's spirit visited you in a dream? That's a little hard for me to believe. Who really told you he was here?"

"I'm telling you Mary, my sister's spirit told me. So, if you don't mind, I'll be taking him home with me."

"Hold on there Francis, before I turn the boy over to you, there's a matter of money."

"What matter of money are we talking about Mary?"

"At least twenty dollars. I've spent that much or more on him."

Francis knew Mary had spent very little money on Uniford. But she opened her purse and handed Mary a twenty-dollar gold piece. She took Uniford back to Mercer County to live with her family, raising him as if he were her own child. If not for her dream she would not have known Uniford had been taken to Washington County. He grew up in his Aunt's house with his twelve cousins.

The Three Sisters

1896

There were three spinster sisters, Bessie, Leona and Cally May Carr who lived down the road from my great Grandmother McCrystal's house. After their parents died, Bessie, the oldest girl, became head of the household. She decided how the money was spent and whom it was spent on. If the fire in the hearth started burning low and the room was getting cold, it was Bessie who decided if another log would be added.

She bossed her sisters around needlessly. If Leona and Cally May didn't do what Bessie told them to do, she would bite them on the arm and pull their hair. She would intentionally break their possessions and blame the incident on them.

Lucille, a woman of color, had worked for the family for thirty years. She pleaded to Mr. Carr before he died to leave Miss Leona, his second daughter, in charge of the household because she was twice as sensible as Miss Bessie. But he refused. He made it clear to Lucille, that Bessie, the oldest daughter would be in charge. Lucille knew that meant trouble but there wasn't anything she could do about it.

One month after the death of their Father, Bessie ruled the roost. Leona and Cally May didn't have any choice about the food they ate, what chores they were to do or when they got to go to town. Those decisions were up to Bessie.

They were allowed to read books by candlelight at night only if Bessie wanted to read too. A single candle, moved closest to Bessie, was used to illuminate three separate books.

"No need in wasting candles, we can all see from this one," Bessie would say in a smurky voice.

The curtains in Leona and Cally May's bedroom were old and tattered, but Bessie's room had brand-new store-bought curtains hanging over her windows. Bessie moved the better pieces of furniture from around the house into her room. Her closet was filled with nightgowns, petticoats, dresses, shoes and hats. Leona and Cally May's closet held the barest of essentials. Two nightgowns apiece, three dresses, and the same hats they had been wearing for a year.

Lucille watched as both Miss Leona and Miss Cally May waned under their sister's domination. There wasn't anything she could do about it except pray.

One winter night the fire burned out and the house was very cold. Leona and Cally May pleaded with Bessie to keep the fire going, but she refused, telling her sister's.

"Go to bed if you're cold. Stop being such complainers."

The next morning, the water in the bowl and pitcher were frozen. Inside the house the windows were frosted over with ice crystals. Lucille was the first one to get up, and she started a fire in the fireplace and another one in the wood cook stove. Normally the two heat sources together warmed the house up in no time. But this morning it seemed to get colder as the fires grew hotter.

Leona and Cally May came into the kitchen with blankets wrapped around them.

"Why is it so cold in the house?" Leona asked Lucille.

"It got mighty cold last night, I suspect the temperature went down below zero outside." Lucille answered.

"Has Bessie gotten up yet?" Cally May asked.

"No, she hasn't, you better go get her up," Lucille replied.

When Leona opened the door to Bessie's room a cold wind blew her hair back. She noticed that a window in Bessie's room was wide open, then looked down at her sister in the bed. A layer of frost covered the blankets and Bessie's face. Thinking her sister was dead, Leona screamed with all of her might.

Cally May and Lucille came running into the bedroom to see what was the matter.

When Lucille saw Bessie, she cringed. When Cally May saw Bessie she screamed, "Is she dead?"

Lucille felt for a pulse on Bessie's neck and found a faint beating of Bessie's heart under her fingers.

"She isn't dead, but hurry, we must warm her up. Miss Leona, close that window!"

They carried Bessie into the kitchen, laying her next to the hearth. Leona stoked the fire with the poker and added more logs. They put hot water bottles between Bessie and her blankets. The house warmed up, but Bessie didn't respond to the heat.

"Why was the window in Bessie's room open?" Leona asked Lucille.

"I have no idea why the window was open in there."

In the afternoon Bessie seemed to feel better, though she was weak and very pale.

"Why am I here in the kitchen?" Bessie asked.

"We are trying to warm you up. Somehow a window in your bedroom was opened during the night. You were almost frozen to death." Lucille told her.

Bessie started beating her fists against the floor and protesting, "Take me to my room, I will not die while I am laying on the kitchen floor."

"Should we go fetch the doctor?" Leona asked Lucille.

"No, it's too cold for any of us to fetch the doctor. We could get lost on the way and die ourselves. Let's take her to her room and try to get her to drink some hot tea, it will warm her up."

Leona and Cally May helped Bessie to her room. Bessie was like a rag doll, dragging her feet behind her.

Lucille brought a cup of hot sassafras tea to the room and handed the cup to Cally May.

"Here Sister, try sipping this," Cally May offered Bessie a drink.

Bessie sipped the hot tea into her mouth but got choked. She coughed and coughed, not able to catch her breath. Leona patted her sister's back to relieve the coughing spell, but Bessie began vomiting blood. They called out to Lucille for help.

When Lucille saw the blood and heard the deep rattle in Bessie's chest, she knew what was wrong. Bessie had pneumonia and she didn't have long to live.

Bessie raised up and said, "I am dying, help me."

They all attempted to comfort her while she was breathing her last breath. Though she had always been mean to them, she was their sister, and Leona and Cally May were worried and scared.

Bessie sat up in her bed and said, "After I die, I want my room to stay just as it is. I don't want you to touch my books, move my furniture or wear my clothes. If you do I will come back to haunt you."

Bessie coughed out a chuck of blood onto her pillow, and died.

They buried her the next day. The ground was frozen so hard it was difficult for the neighbor men to dig her grave. They used a pick to break the ground up in order to complete the job.

Lucille locked the door to Bessie's bedroom, just as Bessie had asked. Whenever Leona and Cally May walked by the bedroom they felt a cold air coming out from under the door.

A few days after the funeral when all the mourners and friends had come and gone and all of the funeral food brought by the neighbors had been eaten, Leona, Cally May and Lucille were sitting in the kitchen talking.

"I suppose you will be charge of the household now Miss Leona." Lucille commented.

"Yes, I suppose so, as soon as the lawyer does the paperwork. I'll have to go to town this week to settle Bessie's estate."

"Can I go with you?" Cally May asked Leona.

"Of course, you can go with me, of course."

"I wish we had something new to wear to town," Cally May commented.

"Maybe we will go shopping for a new dress when we go to town." Leona answered.

Cally May continued, "We could wear one of Bessie's dresses."

"You better not do that," Lucille protested. "Remember what Bessie said about leaving her room just as it is, or she would come back from the dead and haunt us."

"I don't believe she can," Leona replied. "Lucille?" "Where is the key to Bessie's bedroom door?"

"Right here in my pocket."

"Give it to me."

Lucille reluctantly handed the key to Leona.

When Leona opened Bessie's bedroom door, freezing cold air hit her in the face. She shivered.

"The window is open again, how is that possible?" Leona asked. "Lucille, get me a hammer and a few nails and I am going to nail that window shut until springtime comes."

Cally May began going through Bessie's closet.

"Oh, I love this green dress, I have always admired it. May I have it sister?" Cally May asked Leona.

"I would leave Bessie's things alone if I were you." Lucille implied with a stern look on her face.

"You may have the green dress, Cally May."

"Thank you, Leona."

Cally May held the dress up to her body and touched the dressers mirror for a better view of the dress. The mirror cracked into hundreds of little pieces. Cally May jumped backwards then said, "oh my Lord, what caused the mirror to break?"

Lucille answered first, "I'm suspecting it was Miss Bessie."

"What?" Cally May exclaimed.

"It wasn't Bessie." Leona said. "The mirrors surface was very cold, and the touch of your hand was enough to shatter it. It was ready to pop from the slightest jar."

"Are you sure Leona?" Cally May asked.

"I am sure Sister."

Lucille shook her head. She knew trouble was coming.

Leona and Cally May began moving furniture out of Bessie's room. Putting their Grandmother's rocking chair back near the hearth in the front room where it had sat for many years, until Bessie put it her room. They took the curtains down from Bessie's room and hung them in the front parlor's windows. The marble topped table that belonged to their mother was returned to its place in the parlor.

Leona locked the bedroom door back for the night.

"Just in case the window comes open again, the house will stay warmer."

Lucille suspected it was for different reasons.

Cally May ironed her new green dress before she went to bed. Leaving it hanging on a hook in the hallway. When she went to sleep, she dreamed she was wearing the green dress and saw her sister Bessie coming toward her. Bessie threw lit matches at her, catching the dress on fire. Cally May tried to take the dress off but her hands wouldn't move. She felt an extreme wave of heat hit her face and then she screamed.

Leona and Lucille came running in to her.

"Are you having a bad dream?" Leona asked her.

"Yes, it was a terrible dream."

"Do you want to talk about it?"

"Not right now, maybe in the morning."

Leona and Lucille left Cally Mays room. As Lucille walked down the hallway, she tripped over something and fell to the floor.

"Ouch," she said, as she gathered herself up.

"What happened Lucille?" Leona asked.

"I tripped over something."

Leona lit a candle and held it up so that they could see what she had tripped over. It was the green dress, right in the middle of the hallway wadded up into a ball.

"The dress must have fallen off the hook," Leona commented.

"How did it get so wrinkled from just falling off of a hook?" Lucille asked her.

Cally May joined them in the hallway. "What are you looking at?"

"We are looking at the green dress you ironed last night, look at it yourself."

Cally May came closer and upon seeing the dress she began to cry.

"How did my dress get in such a mess?" she asked.

"I would be afraid to say," Lucille answered

After hanging the dress back on the hook, they all went back to bed. The next morning while Lucille was cooking breakfast, she noticed the rocking chair out of the corner of her right eye. It was rocking by itself, a sign of a very bad omen to come.

The chair was cold as ice to her touch as she attempted to make it stop rocking. All of a sudden, the rocker stopped rocking. Lucille didn't like what was happening one bit. She didn't mention the incident to Miss Leona or Miss Cally May because it would only frighten them.

Later that day, Leona went into the parlor. She was expecting Mrs. Sara Terhune to stop by for a visit in the afternoon. When she pulled the curtains open, the material seemed to be rotten as they fell off of the curtain rods that were holding them up.

"Lucille, come here quick."

Lucille looked at Miss Leona's face and knew things weren't right.

"Look at these curtains, there rotten and they've come off of the rods, how is that possible?"

"I wouldn't want to say Miss Leona. I wouldn't want to say."

Just then the marble topped table started moving across the floor. Leona and Lucille watched as it moved toward the hallway.

"Do something Lucille," Leona cried.

Lucille didn't know what to do. Her instincts caused her to grab her bible. She placed it on top of the table and the table stopped moving.

"Oh Lucille, is it true? Is Bessie haunting us because we opened her room?"

"It appears that way Miss Leona."

"Oh Lucille, what shall we do?"

"I think we should put everything back into Miss Bessie's room and lock the door. Maybe that will soothe her spirit."

All of the items taken from Bessie's room were returned there. The furniture, the curtains and the clothes.

On Monday morning Leona and Cally May went to town to see the lawyer about settling Bessie's estate. On the way into Harrodsburg, they saw the cutest little house for sale. It was brick, built in the Federal style. There was a white picket fence and a wonderful brick gazebo in the side yard that would be the perfect place to sit and receive visitors.

Leona inquired about the house to the lawyer during their meeting. When Leona came out of the lawyer's office she asked Cally May, "how would you like to move to town?"

"I would love to move to town Leona, I've always wanted to live in town."

Leona made arrangements to purchase the house in town, and to put their house in the country on the market for sale. The lawyer assured them that it was a smart thing to do.

The two sisters were anxious to tell Lucille about the new house. They asked her to move to town with them and she accepted the invitation.

They took everything with them except for what was in Bessie's room.

Several months later the country house sold. When the new owners opened Bessie's bedroom door, they expected to see the items the previous owners had told them were left there. The bedroom was completely empty. Everyone assumed that gypsy's stole the personal property and took Bessie's spirit with them when they left.

One night, several years later, Leona, Cally May and Lucille were talking. Leona spoke up and said.

"I have a confession to make."

"What is it Leona?" Cally May asked.

"I'm the one who opened the window in Bessie's room that night, I wanted her to get sick and die. Now I am ashamed of myself," Leona proclaimed.

Cally May looked at her Sister and said, "No, it wasn't you who opened the window, it was me, I hoped that Bessie would get sick, then I felt really bad when she died."

"You both are wrong," Lucille said. "I opened the window in Bessie's room that night, it was me. Bessie died because of me."

"It couldn't have been you Lucille, I remember opening the window." Leona insisted.

"No, it was me." Cally May told them both.

"I'm telling you two misses that I am the one who opened the window on that cold night, and I don't want to ever hear about this again. Do you hear me?" Lucille asked.

"Yes, Lucille we hear you."

They never discussed the matter again.

Little Graves

1897

Great Grandpa and Great Grandma Leonard had seven children. Ansel, Harvey D, Claudia, Minnie, Pearlie, Vivian and Maudie. They lived two miles west of Harrodsburg on a one-hundred-acre farm.

Matt Bottom, a freed slave from another farm, lived with Grandma and Grandpa since they were married. The Leonard's were against slavery and never owned any slaves. Matt was considered to be part of their family. He was intelligent, intuitive and superstitious. Matt was a master craftsman. Many pieces of furniture he made are still in the family today.

The main income for the farm was cattle. Every year Grandpa Leonard rode his horse General to Burgin Kentucky while several hired hands drove the cattle to the depot. He left General at the Burgin Livery Stable for the trip home. The cattle were loaded onto train cars to be shipped to Chicago to be sold. Grandpa rode in the drover's caboose for the two-day journey.

The morning Grandpa was scheduled to leave was an unusually hot day for the month of September. But the plans had been made and at 7:00 a.m. he left the farm with the cattle.

His wife, children and Matt wished him well as he headed down the lane.

Matt went to the barn to work and the children followed their Mother back into the house.

Grandma told them, "You all go outside and play for a while."

"There's nothing to do!" Ansel said.

"I can find plenty of chores for you," Grandma told them.

"We will find something to do Mother."

With that being said, all of the children ran out the front door.

Harvey D told his siblings, "I know what we can do. Let's have a pretend funeral. I want to practice my preaching."

"How do we have a pretend funeral?"

"Well, we will make several little graves. Then I can preach over them."

The children got a small shovel from the smokehouse and dug up dirt. They formed the dirt into little mounds in the shape of graves.

Matt noticed the children huddled together on the ground, so he went to see what they were doing.

"What in the world are you doing?"

"We're making little graves."

"Oh, children, you should never do that! If you make a grave before you need it someone will die. Take the shovel right now and destroy those mounds. Say a prayer that everyone will be safe. Never let me find you doing such a thing again, or I will tell your parents."

"We will tear them down. Please don't tell Mother about it, Matt."

"I've got to go over to Mr. Isham's farm. I'll be back in an hour. You make sure these graves are gone before I get back."

"We will Matt. We promise."

Harvey D took the shovel and began to slowly move the dirt.

"I don't see what it could hurt to have a pretend funeral. Matt gets upset over silly things. Besides, I didn't get to practice my preaching."

"I agree with Harvey D. How could this hurt anyone? Let's have the funeral and then we can take the graves apart."

Everyone agreed, except Maudie.

"I don't think we should do it anymore. Matt told us not to."

"If you don't want to do it go sit on the porch. We can have fun without you. Anyway, you don't look very good Maudie."

Maudie left the yard and went to the front porch where she sat down on the swing.

The other children started making the little graves again. The girls made crosses out of sticks tied together with blades of grass and placed them on the graves.

"You all stand in a circle around the graves and I will preach. Dear Lord, welcome these poor souls into heaven. Their time on earth has come to past. Though they were sinners, forgive them their sins. Bless their souls so they can be with you through eternity. Amen, amen."

"That was very good Harvey D. I believe you could be a preacher," Claudia said.

"Time to come in for dinner," Grandma Leonard called from the porch.

The children ran to the house. Maudie was stretched out on the swing.

"Come on Maudie. Mother said dinner was ready."

"I don't want any dinner. I'm not hungry."

"Suit yourself."

"Where's Maudie?"

"She's out there on the swing. She said she didn't want anything to eat."

"Maudie, get on in here and eat your dinner."

Maudie came into the house.

"Maudie, your face is flushed. Are you feeling bad?" Her Mother asked.

"I feel funny Mother. I really don't want anything to eat."

"Let me feel your forehead. Child you are burning up. You must have a fever. Ansel, go get Matt. Tell him to go to the icehouse and bring back a sack of ice. I've got to get Maudie's fever down."

"Matt has gone over to Mr. Isham's farm."

"Well, you go get the ice."

"Yes, Mother."

Grandma put Maudie in her bed and washed her down with rubbing alcohol. The little girl seemed to be losing conscience and Grandma couldn't get her to respond to her.

"Harvey D, I need you to go to town and get the doctor right away. Run as fast as you can."

"Yes, Mother."

Harvey D ran down the lane where he met Matt returning home.

"Mother has sent me to get the doctor. Maudie is sick. Ansel is getting ice to cool her down."

"You go back home. I'll borrow Mr. Isham's horse. That is the quickest way to get to town."

Matt ran back down the lane, Harvey D ran back to the house.

Ansel had brought the ice to the house and Grandma had packed it around Maudie. All of the children were in the bedroom with their Mother.

"Children, say a prayer for your sister. I'm afraid she is very sick. Oh, how I wish your Father was here. There isn't any way to get in touch with him. He is somewhere between Burgin and Chicago. You all go wait on the porch and watch for the doctor."

"Yes, Mother."

The children were upset. The girls were crying.

"Do you suppose we made Maudie sick by making those little graves. Do you think she will die?" Vivian asked.

"Don't be ridiculous. Those little graves didn't have anything to do with Maudie being sick," Harvey D said.

"But Matt said it was a bad omen. We shouldn't have made them." Minnie said.

"Minnie is right. We shouldn't have made those graves. If Maudie dies it will be our fault."

"Don't be so stupid sisters."

Just then, they saw Matt on horseback and the doctor in his buggy coming down the lane.

"Mother, the doctor is here."

Doctor Thompson hurried into the house. Matt stayed on the porch with the children.

"I'm going to water my horse. All of you wait here until I get back."

As Matt led the horse across the yard, he saw the little graves again.

"Ansel, Harvey D, come here now! You didn't destroy the little graves. Instead, you've decorated them. I told you to get rid of them. Now your sister is sick. Do you realize you have probably caused her sickness and possible death by continuing to play with them? What is wrong with you?"

"We didn't think it would hurt anything Matt. We're sorry."

"It's too late to be sorry. Destroy them now."

The boys tore down the little graves and then returned to the porch. They heard Grandma crying.

She came out on the porch.

"Doctor Thompson thinks Maudie has diphtheria. He doesn't know if he can save her life or not. Matt, ride into town and send Harve a telegram at the YMCA in Chicago. He won't be there yet, but the telegram will be there when he arrives."

Matt remounted Mr. Isham's horse and headed back to Harrodsburg.

Doctor Thompson told Grandma Leonard to keep Maudie cool. She needed to attempt to get fluids in Maudie somehow. But when Grandma tried to get Maudie to drink the fluid it ran down her face and neck.

"We will know more in the morning. I'll come back at sunrise."

"Thank you, Doctor."

Grandma sat up all night with Maudie. She sent the children to bed early, but none of them could sleep. They kept thinking about what Matt had said about the little graves.

The next morning Doctor Thompson arrived back at the farm. Maudie wasn't any better. In fact, she was worse.

"I hate to tell you this Mrs. Leonard, but I doubt she lives through the day."

"What will I do doctor? Her Father is in Chicago selling cattle. I sent him a telegram but he probably won't receive it until tonight."

"I'll stay here with you for a while. If Maudie dies, we will be able to get the neighbors to help bury her."

"We can't bury her before her Father returns."

"In this heat, we will have to."

By this time, Grandpa had arrived at the stockyards with his cattle. He had felt uneasy all day. As his cattle went through the selling ring, he heard music. It sounded like music that would be played in a church. He turned to the man seated beside him and said,

"Do you hear music playing?"

"No, I don't hear any music."

"Are you sure?"

"Yes, I'm sure."

Grandpa's cattle sold for the highest price ever. He felt good about the sale results but still had a feeling of dread. As he rode in the back of a buggy to the hotel, he heard music playing again. He later would describe it as sounding celestial.

When he reached the hotel, the clerk gave him the telegram that Grandma had sent. He became terribly upset. There wasn't anyway he could get back to Kentucky in less than two days. He would have to collect his money for the cattle the next afternoon. The check wouldn't be ready before then. That meant he would miss the train for tomorrow. It would be the next day before he could leave Chicago.

He sent Grandma a telegram saying he had received hers and he would be back as soon as he could be. Before he went to sleep, he heard the music playing again.

Though Grandpa didn't know it, Maudie had died that afternoon. They took her body to Dixville and buried her at the church's cemetery.

The Leonard children were beside themselves. Every one of them had come to believe they had killed their sister. They were afraid to mention the fact to their Mother and hoped that Matt wouldn't tell her about the little graves.

Two days later Grandpa returned from Chicago. Matt met him at the depot and informed him that Maudie had died and been buried at Dixville.

"I will never see my little girl again," Grandpa cried.

"You will see her again. I assure you of that," Matt told him.

Grandpa regretted that Maudie had been buried at Dixville. He wished she had been buried at Bruner's Chapel Church Cemetery instead.

Nine months after Maudie's death, Grandpa decided to have her body moved to Bruner's Chapel. Several men, along with Grandpa and Matt took a horse and a wagon to Dixville to get the body.

When they had dug up the casket, Grandpa wanted to open the casket to see Maudie's body.

"No, Mr. Leonard, you don't want to do that. Her body will have decomposed by now. It would be a gruesome sight. Remember your daughter as she was when she was alive."

"No, I want to see her again."

"I've got a feeling it will be all right. Go ahead, open the casket," Matt said.

Reluctantly the men opened the casket. Grandpa looked down at the body, then fell to the ground. Matt helped him up and they both looked at Maudie's body at the same time.

Her body was in near perfect condition. She looked like she was sleeping. Even the flower in her hand still had petals on it.

"How is that possible?" One of the men asked.

"Maudie and God wanted me to see her one last time. That's why she hasn't decomposed. She was waiting for me to see her. It was meant to me."

Grandpa kissed Maudie and the men closed the casket. They put the casket on the wagon and took Maudie to Bruner's Chapel.

Grandma Leonard was waiting there with her other children. Maudie's casket was lowered into the newly dug grave and covered over with dirt.

On the way back home, the children talked among themselves.

"We killed Maudie, didn't we?"

"Yes, I believe we did."

"How can we ever forgive ourselves?"

"We can't forgive ourselves. We won't ever be able to."

The Pocket Watch

1897

In 1874 Great Grandpa McCrystal dug a new well for Mr. Thomas Colby. It took him two weeks to complete the project since the clay dirt was hard as a rock.

Mr. Colby promised my Grandpa twenty dollars for doing the job. A large sum of money for two weeks work in those days.

When payday came, Mr. Colby didn't have the full amount of money.

He told Grandpa, "About the money, Mr. McCrystal, the twenty dollars I promised you, I don't have it."

"Excuse me sir, but we had a deal. Full payment upon completion of the job."

"I know, but I don't have the whole twenty dollars, I have eleven dollars I'll give you now."

"But sir, we had an agreement. The amount was twenty dollars."

"I understand the agreement was for twenty dollars, Mr. McCrystal, but I'm telling you I only have eleven dollars. Old Man Taylor was supposed to come buy three geese from me, but he didn't show up, I was counting on that money to pay you."

"I'm sorry about your misfortunes, Mr. Colby, but my wife is expecting me to bring twenty dollars home tonight and if I don't have it, she'll have a fit. Could you pay the other nine dollars on Monday?"

"No, I'm afraid not Mr. McCrystal," Mr. Colby hung his head in shame.

"What I will do is give you my old pocket watch; it runs good. I tell you, Mr. McCrystal this watch would sell for twenty dollars in town. Here look for yourself."

Mr. Colby handed the pocket watch to Grandpa.

Grandpa looked it over. It was a Waltham pocket watch in a gold-filled case with an eagle embossed on it. He pressed the knob on top of the watch and the case opened immediately. Grandpa liked it. Holding it made him feel special.

"Mr. Colby, it's a deal. But if my wife runs me off when I get home can I spend a couple of nights in your barn?"

"Sure Mr. McCrystal, be glad for you to."

The pocket watch was Grandpa's most prized possession for the rest of his life. If the watch wasn't in the pocket of his pants, it was in the top drawer of the cherry chest.

Years later when Grandpa died the family wanted to bury the watch with him, but they couldn't find it. They searched everywhere in the house, but it was never found.

The cherry chest was handed down to the next generation to Grandpa's oldest daughter, Sarah, who decided to have her husband refinish the chest. She wanted it to look as it did when she when was a little girl and watched her Mother fold her clothes away into those very drawers.

When Tom started to remove the drawers, the top drawer was stuck. He worked it back and forth several times until he heard something fall and hit the floor. When he scooted the chest away from the wall, he was surprised to see what he saw.

"Of all things," he said to his wife.

"What is it?"

"It's Grandpa's old pocket watch. It must have been stuck in the back of the drawer. He was always so proud of it."

"I thought they buried it with him."

"No, we couldn't find the watch anywhere when he died. Don't you remember?"

"Now that you mention it, I do remember. Someone said they thought it had been stolen after we couldn't find it anywhere."

He held the watch up so that his wife could see it.

"Papa wouldn't want you to carry his watch around."

"I don't have to carry it. I'll leave it on the mantel. Papa would like that."

"Yes, I suppose he would."

Tom took a piece of cedar and whittled a stand. He shined the watch and placed it in the stand on the mantel. He stood back to admire his work.

"I think Papa would be happy to see his watch displayed on the mantel. It looks real nice up there."

"Yes, it does."

The next morning, Uncle Tom saw the pocket watch wasn't in its stand.

"Did you move the watch?" he asked.

"No, I didn't move it, it's there on the mantel."

"The stand is here, but the watch isn't."

"That's strange. Did it fall to the floor?"

"It's not on the floor. Where is it?"

"Did you put it back in the cherry chest?"

"No, I didn't put it back in the drawer. Why would I do that?"

"Maybe you did it by mistake. Just go look in the drawer."

When Uncle Tom opened the drawer, he said, "You are trying to fool me, aren't you?"

"Trying to fool you about what?"

He reached in the drawer and brought Grandpa's pocket watch out.

"You must have put the watch back in the drawer."

"I didn't put the watch in the drawer. When I went to bed last night it was on the mantel in the stand."

"Well, it didn't get there by itself!"

"Just tell me you put the watch back in the drawer. I won't be mad."

"I'm telling you for the last time. I didn't put the watch in the drawer."

"When we go to bed tonight, I'm going to make sure the watch is on the mantel. I'm telling you that!"

They returned the watch to the stand on the mantel and made sure it was there before they went to bed.

The next morning the watch wasn't on the mantle. They found it back in the drawer.

"Someone's playing tricks on me, they have to be," Tom said.

"It doesn't make any sense at all. Maybe you moved it back there while you were sleeping."

Tom gave Sarah a disgusted look. He returned the watch to the mantel.

That night Uncle Tom decided to sleep in the kitchen to keep an eye on the watch. He tied a thin piece of string from the base of the mantel over to his finger. If anyone or anything attempted to remove the watch from the stand, the string would pull his finger and wake him up.

Sometime during the night Uncle Tom awoke. He saw Aunt Sarah standing in the kitchen. She was wearing what looked to be a man's suit.

"What are you doing up? And why are you wearing that outfit?"

She didn't answer him. She turned and walked into the other bedroom.

When Tom opened his eyes the next morning he looked directly toward the mantel. The watch was gone from the stand.

Aunt Sarah came into the kitchen.

"What were you doing up in the middle of the night?"

"I wasn't up in the middle of the night. What are you talking about?"

"I saw you standing here in the kitchen. You had on my suit!"

"That's ridiculous! Why would I be wearing your suit?"

"Well, maybe I dreamed it. It sure seemed real."

"You must have."

"The pocket watch isn't on the mantel. I figure its back in the drawer."

"Let's look."

Aunt Sarah went to the cherry chest of drawers and pulled out the top drawer. The watch was there.

"You know what this means?"

"No, what does it mean?"

"It means I saw Grandpa's spirit in the kitchen last night. He wants his watch in the drawer, not on the mantel. His spirit moved the watch back where it belongs. You know if the watch wasn't in his pocket, it was in the chest. We couldn't find the watch to bury with him, so, if it's not in his pocket, it should be in the drawer."

"I think you are right."

The pocket watch stayed in the drawer for many more years until, sadly, the chest and watch were lost in a fire.

In Agreement

1897

When my Mother, Rosa Henry, was a little girl, she became very sick. She had symptoms of a fever, but no fever. She cried out for water, but refused to drink. Her body was as limp as a rag doll. It seemed she was in a trance and unaware of her surroundings.

All morning she thrashed around in her bed, fighting her Mother and her Aunts Mag and Bess when they tried to comfort her. She waved her arms in the air and kicked her feet.

They were very worried when they washed her face with a wet cloth and patted her cheeks, but she wouldn't open her eyes. It was as if she couldn't wake up.

By early afternoon they sent their neighbor, Randell Claunch to town to bring Doctor Temple to the farm. Randell rode his mule Sassy quickly out of the yard.

A good hour passed before Randell returned with the doctor.

"Randell said Rosa won't wake up. It sounds serious, ladies. Take me to her right now."

"Yes, Doctor; she's in her bedroom."

They were surprised to see her hair wet from sweating. Doctor Temple slipped a thermometer into her mouth.

"Her temperature is one hundred and three. Her pulse rate is too high for a young child. We've got to cool her body down."

He opened her eyes and shined a light into them.

"I'm afraid Rosa might have Typhoid Fever."

"Oh no, Doctor, not Typhoid Fever, that could kill her!"

"Yes, it could kill her. The fever has made its way around the county. Has Rosa had any bad water to drink?"

"No Doctor, our well is clean."

"Has she visited anyone that could have bad water?"

"She hasn't visited anyone at all lately."

"I heard the Johnson children have Typhoid. Is that true Doctor?"

"Yes, I'm afraid so. Four of the Johnson children have died from it."

"Four children have died. What can we do Doctor?"

"We will have to get her fever down. Do you have any ice?"

"There might be a little ice in the root cellar."

"Get it right away. We will pack it around her body to cool her down."

Aunt Mag went immediately and brought back a dish pan full of it.

"Ladies, put the ice all around Rosa's body. Try to get her to drink some water. You should also open the window to keep fresh air in the room."

"What else can we do Doctor?"

"You can pray. We will know in the next twenty-four hours if Rosa will live or die. There's nothing else I can do."

The women were besides themselves, they prayed through their tears.

"Rosa cannot die. I wouldn't be able to live without her. We must pray harder, Sisters. Pray to God, pray to Mary, pray to everyone we know that's in Heaven."

Aunt Bess got Rosa a glass of water and tried to get her to drink. It ran out the sides of her mouth. Finally they used a glass straw that allowed a small amount of water to seep into her mouth. They prayed until midnight for Rosa's recovery.

The women took turns sitting up with Rosa. Aunt Bess was first, covering herself with a summer quilt.

Rosa continued to thrash her legs and arms violently. She pulled her own hair and talked crazy.

Around midnight Aunt Mag came so Aunt Bess could rest.

"Bess, you go lie down for a while, I'll watch her."

"O.K.," Bess answered in a yawn. "I'm worried about her Mag. She's talking out of her head."

"What did she say?"

"Nothing she has said made any sense. She said, "I like your green apron, and I didn't know your hair was red."

"She must be dreaming."

"Maybe she is. It's probably just fever talk."

"Let's just try to keep Rosa comfortable. Dr. Temple will be back in the morning. Hopefully she'll be better by then."

"I sure hope so."

"Here, the blanket is still warm, cozy up in it, Mag."

Rosa turned over on the bed and Aunt Mag thought the child's face looked flushed. So, she laid a wet washcloth across Rosa's forehead. The little girl seemed to sigh with relief, and so did Aunt Mag.

Aunt Mag didn't remember when she dozed off. She swore she never fell asleep, until she was startled by Rosa calling her name.

"Aunt Mag, Aunt Mag, why are you sitting in that rocking chair? Why aren't you in bed?"

The child seemed to make perfect sense.

"Well, sweet child, you've been sick, and I was watching over you. How are you feeling now?"

"I feel fine Aunt Mag, I haven't been sick."

"We had Doctor Temple come to see you. He was concerned about you and so were we."

"I'm not sick. I've been asleep. I know it's the middle of night, but I'm hungry. Would you get me a bite of something please?"

"Of course, Rosa. I'll be right back."

Aunt Mag woke her sisters.

"Rosa is feeling better; she wants something to eat."

"Praise the Lord," they said.

Several biscuits were left from supper, so Aunt Bess sliced them, and filled them with butter and apple jelly, Rosa's favorite.

"Oh, Sweetheart I'm so glad you are feeling better."

"I feel fine, Mom; I don't remember being sick. Aunt Mag said Doctor Temple had been here to see me, and that he was concerned. I don't think I had a condition, Mom; I was just sleeping."

"You're better now and that's what matters. We sure were worried about you."

"I'll tell you what I do remember."

"What Rosa, what do you remember?" Aunt Bess asked.

"The dream I had while I was asleep."

"What was your dream about?"

"Well, I was flying through the air like a bird. I soared way up in the sky, then I swooped down. I flew over our farm and I saw the house and the barn and the pond. It was exciting!"

Rosa continued, "I saw a bright light up in the sky. It was higher than I had flown before. There was something about that light that made me want to fly up to it. I flapped my arms, and in no time, I reached the bright light. I had this feeling in my body, like small sparks of fire were hitting my skin. It made me shiver, then I got scared. I went on toward the bright light because I thought I heard someone calling my name. Right then, I did hear someone calling my name. They were saying, "Rosa, Rosa, turn around and don't go any farther. Listen to me. I turned to see who was talking to me."

"Who was it?" Aunt Mag asked.

"It was the lady whose picture is on the mantel, your Grandmother, Mom."

"What?" everyone asked in a surprised voice.

"I'm telling you, Mom. It was the lady in the picture on the mantel."

"That is a picture of your Great-Grandmother Peavler."

"I know, Mom, but she looked different then she does in the picture."

"What do you mean?" Aunt Bess asked her.

"Well, her hair was different; it was red, not grey, like in the picture. But I recognized her."

The women looked at one another with eerie feelings.

"What else do you remember, Rosa?"

"She was wearing a pretty green apron over her dress. She patted something against her leg. I think it was a wooden spoon. Yes, it was a wooden spoon. She shook it at me when she told me to leave the light. She said it wasn't my time to be there and I needed to leave and come back here to the house. In fact, she insisted. She tapped the spoon against her leg and at first, I was scared of her. But when she smiled at me, I wasn't afraid anymore. As I flew away from the light, I heard her giggle. It was a silly giggle, going up and down. Then she started to sing."

"What song was she singing, Rosa?"

"Oh, that song I've heard you sing before Mom. You know, "What you going to do when the well runs dry, Honey? What you going do when the well runs dry Babe? What you going to do when the well runs dry? Sit on the banks and cry, cry, cry, Honey, Baby mine. I like that song, Mom."

"I know you do."

"I heard her singing it until I landed back on the earth and woke up here in my bed."

Aunt Bess handed Rosa the biscuits with apple jelly. She ate them right away and drank a glass of warm milk.

"Mom, I think I'll go back to sleep."

"All right, Rosa, good night. We'll see you in the morning."

They each kissed her forehead, closed the bedroom door and went into the kitchen to talk.

"How could she know those things about Grandma Peavler?" Aunt Mag asked.

"How did she know that Grandma had red hair? I've never mentioned it to her; had no need to. Besides, the picture on the mantel is in black and white, and, as far as I know, that's the only picture of Grandma Peavler that exists."

"What about the green apron? When Rosa was sick, she said she liked someone's green apron."

"Grandma Peavler always wore a green apron. Green was her favorite color. Rosa couldn't have known."

"And what about the spoon?"

"I remember getting smacked on my legs with that wooden spoon."

"So do I."

"Me too!"

"Grandma Peavler tapped the spoon against her leg, knowing it struck fear in all of us. I guess she wanted us to know it was available quickly if she needed it for a spanking."

"I thought getting spanked with the wooden spoon hurt more than a green tree switch."

"It did hurt worse."

"You have to admit she could make her point. Her voice was very determined."

"Yes, it was."

"Then when you minded her, she would smile that sweet smile."

"I can see that smile now."

"So can I."

"You know, Rosa wasn't born when Grandma died. I know we've talked about Grandma in front of her. It's possible we mentioned her red hair, isn't it?"

"I guess we could have mentioned it to her, but I don't remember it."

"What about the green apron, have we ever talked about it?"

"Maybe."

"Have we talked about the wooden spoon, or how she tapped it against her leg?"

"I don't know; it's all strange."

"Rosa never heard Grandma Peavler's silly giggle. Her giggles were funny enough to make you laugh."

"Yes, they were."

"What about the song? Grandma loved that song, and sang it all the time."

"Sisters, my daughter was sick and now she is well. If Grandma Peavler saved Rosa's life and sent her back to earth, so be it I say."

Her sisters agreed.

Around The Bend

1910

A young couple, Stewart and Mary Grace Hardin, left Springfield
in their shiny new buggy headed to Harrodsburg to visit Mary
Grace's elderly aunt, Miss Tolly Pulliam.

Skies were clear that morning, but the temperature was hot for
May. Mary Grace, a slim, blonde-haired beauty, held her parasol at an
angle to shield her husband Stewart from the sun. As they made their
way down Mackville Road they heard a crack of lightning and the
rumble of thunder. Before they knew it, a fierce thunderstorm had
enveloped them.

Stewart noticed an open tobacco barn ahead and quickly drove the
buggy into the center aisle.

"My dress and shoes are wet, Stewart. My hair is a mess. What are
we going to do?"

"You look beautiful to me, Mary Grace. Don't worry. The storm
will pass and we can continue on to Harrodsburg. It's barely past noon;
we have plenty of time."

The storm continued for well over an hour. The rain hit the tin
roof of the barn so loud it spooked their horse, Poppie, a fine boned
bay Standardbred that could trot all day.

Finally, the storm passed, the sun came out, and the birds sang again. Stewart drove the buggy out of the barn and back onto the road.

They had gone about a mile when they came upon an uprooted red oak tree that blocked the road.

"Oh my, Stewart. What do we do now?"

"I believe we can go around the tree through that field, Mary Grace."

"Do you really Stewart?"

"Yes, Sweetheart, please don't worry."

He turned the horse and buggy and drove straight into the field. They hadn't gone ten feet when Stewart realized he had made a mistake. The buggy's wheels sank into the mud. Stewart urged Poppie to pull the buggy through the mud, but the horse's feet slipped from under him. He couldn't get any traction.

"Stewart, do something. Look how muddy the buggy is."

"Whoa there, Poppie, Whoa." The horse stopped pulling.

"Mary Grace, I'll carry you over to the road, then I'll get the buggy out of the field."

"Oh, Stewart, I am scared."

"There's no need to be scared. We'll be on our way in no time."

Stewart carried Mary Grace to the road. She climbed through the limbs of the red oak tree to the other side and waited for her husband.

At first, Stewart tried driving the buggy out of the field, but mud flew everywhere and the buggy sank deeper.

"This isn't going to work," he thought to himself.

He climbed out of the buggy and onto Poppie's back.

"Come on Poppie. Pull," Stewart kicked the horse's flanks, but Poppie still slipped on the mud. After several more attempts the horse managed to pull the buggy out.

"Oh, thank goodness," Mary Grace sighed, "Look at you, you're covered in mud."

"I know it, Sweetheart. There's a creek at the bottom of the next hill. We can clean ourselves up there."

"I think I'll walk to the bottom Stewart, if you don't mind."

"That's fine, Sweetheart. I'll walk with you and lead Poppie."

"I'm starting to think we should have gone back to Springfield after the storm, Stewart."

"We're almost to Mackville now."

"Are you sure Stewart?"

"Yes, I'm sure."

When they reached the creek, Stewart removed his boots and socks and led Poppie and the buggy right into the water. He washed Poppie down first, then the buggy, then himself.

Mary Grace waited on the bank. She washed the mud from her hands and face with her handkerchief.

Within no time they arrived in Mackville. Several people were standing in front of the grocery store.

"Good afternoon gentlemen."

"Good afternoon to you. Where are you headed to this stormy day?"

"We're headed to Harrodsburg. We hope the road is clear. We've already encountered one downed tree today."

"It's clear between here and Jenkensville. I just came from there."

"Oh, that's good to know. You folks have a nice day. My wife and I need to be going."

Stewart and Mary Grace waved at the men as they drove away.

"Stewart, it's getting dark early."

"It's just cloudy from the storm, that's all."

"It's only eight miles to Rose Hill. Poppie will get us there in no time."

She slipped her arm through his for courage and comfort.

Poppie trotted at a good pace and the trip seemed to pass quicker.

Stewart's face brightened as he said, "See, there's old man Peterson's house. We're closer to Rose Hill than I thought. Let's see if he's home."

"No, Stewart. We need to be on our way to town, Mr. Peterson will talk your leg off."

"That's true. He will. We'll stop here on our return trip."

Stewart clucked to Poppie to pick up his pace and the horse responded immediately, going from a fast walk to a trot. As they rounded a bend, the buggy's wheel hit loose gravel that had washed down the hillside. The buggy's wheels started to spin.

"Hold onto me," Stewart called to Mary Grace.

The buggy skidded off the road and hit a tree. Three spokes broke out of the right front wheel.

Mary Grace began to cry. "Stewart, Stewart, were you hurt?"

"No, Sweetheart, I'm fine. But I can't say the same for the buggy's wheel."

Stewart examined the broken spokes and realized he didn't have any way to fix them.

"What are we going to do now?" Mary Grace pleaded.

"I'll unhitch Poppie from the buggy and leave it here. That wheel won't last to the top of the next hill."

"Then what, Stewart?"

"I'll lead Poppie. You can ride him. There's a house just up the road, I'm positive."

Stewart helped Mary Grace onto Poppie's back.

"I'm not comfortable up here, Stewart. It's not proper for me to straddle a horse this way."

"Settle down Mary Grace. You don't have to straddle Poppie's back; just sit sideways. You'll be fine."

"Aunt Tolly will be worried that we haven't arrived yet."

"There's nothing we can do about it now, Sweetheart. We'll explain the situation when we get there."

Thirty minutes passed as they slowly made their way toward Harrodsburg. Somewhere behind them they heard a clap of lightning and terrific thunder.

"Oh no, Stewart, another storm is coming."

"Look sweetheart, there's a house down that driveway. Maybe we can seek refuge from the storm there."

Stewart led Poppie and his wife down the driveway.

"Hello, is anyone home?" Stewart called.

"Yes, we're home," came a reply.

A thin elderly gentleman with long white hair stepped out on the front porch.

"You young folks need to come in here. There's a storm coming. Go put that fine-looking horse of yours in a stall in the barn."

"Oh, thank you, kind sir," Mary Grace said, as Stewart helped her down.

Mary Grace explained their dilemma to the old man.

"We've had a terrible day, sir. We left Springfield six hours ago. We're on our way to visit my aunt in Harrodsburg. I mailed her a post card last week telling her we would be there today. But after getting caught in the storm, we got stuck in the mud. Then the buggy skidded on gravel, hit a tree, and broke three spokes. Now another storm is coming. I don't know what we are going to do," Mary Grace cried.

"Calm down, Sweetheart. We'll be safe here," Stewart said.

"What in the world?" Came a sweet voice inside the house.

An elderly lady wearing a homespun dress and seed sack apron held the screen door.

"My goodness, child, come in."

Mary Grace looked at Stewart.

"Go ahead, Mary Grace. I'll be right in."

"Thank you, ma'am," Mary Grace replied.

"I'll put the horse in the barn, Sweetheart. Then I'll be right there," Stewart said, as he led the horse away. The elderly man followed.

"Your wife mentioned you broke the spokes on your buggy's wheel."

"Yes, sir, we did. By the way, my name is Stewart Hardin. That's my wife Mary Grace."

"Nice to meet you Mr. Hardin. My name is Vernon Carpenter. That's my wife Elenore. Mr. Hardin, where is your buggy now?"

"It's down the road about a mile. Maybe, after this storm passes, I could borrow a few tools and attempt to fix the spokes, Mr. Carpenter."

"Of course, you can. I believe I have some wheel spokes."

"That would be wonderful, Mr. Carpenter. I'll pay you for the supplies."

"I wouldn't hear of that, Mr. Hardin. It's my pleasure to help you young folks. Besides, we don't have any need for money."

"Thank you, Mr. Carpenter."

"I suppose you young folks need to stay for supper. Elenore and I caught some nice brims in the pond out back of the barn this afternoon. We have more than enough."

"We wouldn't want to put you out sir."

"It's no trouble at all. We don't get much company anymore. Seems like no one ever comes to see us, not even our children. I know Elenore would enjoy having you and your wife for supper."

"Well, if you insist, we will accept your fine offer for supper."

A gust of wind blew the barn door shut and caused Stewart and Poppie to jump.

"My goodness, boy, we better head to the house."

"Yes, sir."

The rain poured before they reached the porch.

"Stewart, hurry," Mary Grace called.

The two men hurried into the house and shook the rain off of their hats and jackets.

"Stewart, Mrs. Carpenter has asked us to stay for supper. I told her we would accept her kind invitation."

Stewart and Mr. Carpenter smiled.

The fried fish was delicious. Mrs. Carpenter fried it over an open fire in the stone fireplace. She made corn bread in her iron skillet and sliced it into pie shaped wedges. Diced onions added to fried potatoes filled the house with smells that would drive a hungry man crazy.

"After the storm passes, we will go fix that wheel of yours. Remind me to bring my mallet. It's in the barn."

"I hate for you to help me with the buggy wheel, Mr. Carpenter. There's mud all over the buggy and the wheels."

"Won't take no for an answer, boy. Your wife can stay here with Elenore while we're gone. I've fixed buggy and wagon wheel spokes all my life. People always said I had a certain knack for it. Didn't they Elenore?"

"Yes, Vernon, people always said you had a knack for it."

The storm passed toward the east and the light of day faded into the west. The men found the spokes and mallet in the barn and walked to where the buggy sat.

Stewart watched in amazement as Mr. Carpenter drove the spokes into the hub of the wheel. He had never seen anyone who made such a perfect strike with a mallet. Each spoke went directly into the wheel's hub as if they had been made for it.

"What are the chances that these spokes would fit my wheel?" Stewart asked Mr. Carpenter.

"We got lucky boy; we got lucky."

Stewart and Mr. Carpenter pulled the buggy back to the house as the sun set.

"How much farther is it to Harrodsburg, Mr. Carpenter?"

"You're four miles from town, boy."

"You know, I usually judge the distance by the amount of time on the road, but today, we've been on the road forever. I sort of lost track of our exact location."

"It's an easy thing to do, boy. Especially when you are faced with one problem after another. I wouldn't suggest you drive to town tonight. With these storms going through, there could be trees down between here and Harrodsburg. You need to stay here with Elenore and me tonight."

"Oh, no, sir, that's asking too much," Stewart said.

"No, it's not boy. I told you we would enjoy the company. Nobody ever comes to see us anymore and we get lonesome. Just having you all eat supper with us made Elenore so happy. I could see it in her eyes."

"I'll have to ask Mary Grace."

"Come on, boy, let's go ask her."

"Mary Grace, Mary Grace," Stewart called as they entered the yard.

His wife appeared on the porch, calling to him.

"Stewart, Mrs. Carpenter has asked us to spend the night here. It's almost dark and I'm afraid to head to town. Can we stay here for the night?"

The men looked at each other and smiled.

They sat around the kitchen table and talked. Stewart and Mary Grace told the Carpenters about their home in Springfield. Mary Grace spoke proudly and said,

"Stewart is Vice President of The Springfield National Bank."

The Carpenters were impressed. "A Vice President at your young age," Elenore said. "How wonderful."

"Stewart works very hard at the bank. He is a wonderful mathematician."

"Do you folks have any children?" Elenore asked.

"Not yet, but we are hoping to," she replied with a giggle.

"Does Mr. Ben Camden still operate the general store in Springfield?" Vernon asked.

"Where was his store located, Mr. Carpenter?"

"His store sat right across the street from the courthouse. It had a big sign painted across the front of the building that read, 'Camden's General Store.'"

"I can't seem to place the store, Mr. Carpenter. It seems like I recall my Grandfather mentioning it, but I don't think it's there anymore."

"We once attended an outdoor revival at the First Baptist Church on Spring Street. It was a small church, but they were talking about building a new church. The preacher was a man by the name of Pastor John White. Is he still preaching?" Elenore asked.

"I don't believe he is," Stewart answered.

"Well, it's been several years since we've been to Springfield. Hasn't it, Vernon?"

"Yes, Elenore, it has been a while since we went to Springfield."

Stewart and Mary Grace could tell the Carpenters were getting tired. People in the country go to bed when the sun goes down and the sun had been down for over an hour.

"If you would be kind enough to show us where we can sleep, we'll go to bed now."

"You young folks can sleep in that room over there," Mrs. Carpenter continued, "There's a pitcher of fresh water and a bowl for you to wash up. You can use the cotton towels hanging on the washstand. I laid a clean cotton gown out for you, Honey, and a long nightshirt for you, Stewart."

"Thank you very much, Ma'am. Please let us pay you for all your trouble."

"We wouldn't hear of it. As I told you before, Elenore and I ain't got the need for any money."

"Then goodnight to you both," Stewart said as he closed the bedroom door.

"Oh, Stewart, I am so tired I barely feel like washing my face. I'm going to change into the gown first."

"Mary Grace, I wonder how long it has been since the Carpenters have been to Springfield? They spoke as if it hadn't been that long ago since they attended the revival, and that the church was small. But, if you remember, we went to the fiftieth anniversary of the church building last summer. I still have the program with the history and, as I remember it was built around 1845. That was fifty-two years ago."

"That would mean the Carpenters haven't been to Springfield in over fifty years. That seems strange, doesn't it?" Mrs. Carpenter talked as if it had just been several years."

"Well, I suppose when you get older, time passes faster."

"I suppose."

"Mr. Carpenter told me his children don't come to visit them. Don't you find that odd?"

"Maybe they live somewhere far away."

Mary Grace held up the gown.

"This nightgown must be fifty years old. It's made of muslin. No one wears muslin gowns anymore. Stewart? Did you notice how it smells smoky here? This gown smells smoky. Even the bed linens smell smoky. But I'm so tired I don't care."

"Now that you mentioned it, Mary Grace, everything does smell smoky. When Mr. Carpenter was repairing the wheel, I noticed he smelled smoky, too. Another thing I noticed about him was his boots. They were both made for the same foot. You know, like they use to make shoes. Before there was a right shoe and a left shoe. The Carpenters are an old couple. They are from another generation, that's for sure."

Stewart continued, "This nightshirt is as stiff as a board. It's clean but it seems rotten. I hope I don't rip a hole in it while I'm sleeping."

The couple slept well, and woke at first daylight. They got dressed, made up the bed, and folded their night clothes across the back of a straight chair.

Stewart opened the bedroom door and expected to see the Carpenters in the kitchen, but the house was quiet.

"Wonder where they are?" Mary Grace asked.

"Probably outside," he answered. They stepped out on the front porch.

"Mr. Carpenter, Mr. Carpenter, where are you?" Stewart called. There was no answer.

"Maybe they are fishing. Mary Grace, you wait here. I'll walk out to the pond."

She waited on the porch for her husband to return.

Stewart came back shortly with a strange look on his face.

"What's the matter?" She asked him.

"The pond is dried up. Even the cat tails are dead."

"There must be another pond somewhere on the property, Stewart. Did you look around?"

"I looked around, but I didn't see another pond. I'll go get Poppie hitched up."

"We can't just leave without thanking them, Stewart. That wouldn't be proper."

"I know it. I tell you what, write them a note and put it on the kitchen table. Do you have your paper pad and lead pencil with you?'"

"Yes, I do," Mary Grace answered.

"Here's a silver dollar. Put it with the note. Even though Mr. Carpenter said they didn't have any need for money, everyone has a need for money."

Mary Grace wrote the note while Stewart went into the barn. He found Poppie eating on a fresh bale of hay. He hitched the horse to the buggy, and led Poppie to Mary Grace.

"Let's get going. Did you finish the note?'"

"Yes, I put the note and money on the kitchen table. I feel bad we can't thank them in person."

"On our way back home, we'll stop and see them again. All right Sweetheart?"

"Yes, Stewart, thank you. You know I always want to do the proper thing."

"I know you do. That's one reason I love you so much."

He leaned over and kissed his wife.

Stewart and Mary Grace climbed into the buggy and headed back to the main road.

"I didn't realize how long the driveway was. How did we ever see the Carpenter's house in the first place?" Stewart asked.

"I don't know," she said, shaking her head.

Around the bend and down the road, Poppie trotted up a hill. There ahead, Stewart and Mary Grace saw two men walking along, headed to the fields to work. One was an older man with snow-white hair and the younger man was dark-headed with sunburned arms. Both men were wearing bib overalls and straw hats.

"Whoa, Poppie, whoa. How are you men this fine morning?" Stewart asked.

"Fine, sir, fine," the men answered.

"My wife and I are headed to Harrodsburg."

"Where are you folks from?" The older man asked.

"We're from Springfield," Mary Grace answered.

"My name is Stewart Hardin. This is my wife, Mary Grace."

"Nice to meet you. I'm Mr. Henry and this is my son Richard. You sure must have left Springfield awful early to have made it this far."

"Actually, we left yesterday," Stewart said, "we ran into all kinds of trouble. We were caught in the first storm yesterday afternoon. Then I got the buggy stuck in a field while going around a fallen tree."

"It was terrible," Mary Grace added.

"Then our buggy hit gravel, swerved, and the wheel hit a tree. It broke three spokes out of the wheel's hub."

"How did you get your spokes fixed?" The older gentleman asked.

"Mr. Carpenter fixed it. If it hadn't been for Mr. and Mrs. Carpenter, Mary Grace and I would have been stuck outside all night."

"Who did you say helped you out?"

"Mr. and Mrs. Vernon Carpenter. They live down the road, right around the bend. You are bound to know them."

"You must be mistaken young man. There's no one named Carpenter that lives down the road anymore. You must be talking about Old Man Peterson."

"I know Mr. Peterson sir. My wife and I didn't stop at his house. We stopped at the Carpenter's house. Right around the bend."

"My husband is telling you the truth, gentlemen. We ate a supper of fresh caught brim with the Carpenters. We spent the night in their house. Yesterday afternoon Mr. Carpenter repaired the wheel spoke on the buggy. Told us he had knack for it, didn't he Stewart?"

"Yes, Mary Grace, he did tell us that."

Stewart continued, "Gentlemen, Mr. Carpenter drove a wheel spoke faster than anyone I've ever seen. He had some spokes in his barn that just happened to fit my hub."

The older man spoke, "O.K., that's enough, you two better be on your way. I don't know what kind of trick you are playing, but I don't like it."

"Sir, I assure you, we aren't playing a trick on you. Why would we do that?"

"This here land was my Grandpa Henry's. I've lived here all my life. That house around the bend burned down fifty years ago. The old couple, the Carpenters, that lived there burned up in the fire."

"We can't be speaking of the same place, sir," Stewart told the men.

"There's not another house between here and Mr. Peterson's farm, I'm telling you, boy."

"Sir, far be it from me to ever question my elders. But my wife and I stayed there last night. If you gentlemen have a few minutes, I'll drive us all around the bend to show you I am not a liar."

The two men put their tools down and climbed into the buggy.

"Another thing gentlemen, my horse stayed in a stall in the barn. This morning I found Poppie eating on a nice bale of hay."

"Well, young sir, in only a minute this mystery will be solved."

At first, Stewart couldn't find the driveway. "It's right around here," he told his passengers.

"There it is, Stewart," Mary Grace said, pointing the way.

Stewart turned the buggy onto the overgrown lane.

"I'll have to admit, this seems very peculiar. The Carpenter's driveway wasn't overgrown like this. Was it Mary Grace?"

"No, Stewart, it wasn't."

Mr. Henry spoke up. "Folks, you must have gotten hold of some bad liquor. You are not thinking clearly."

"We are not drinkers sir," Stewart insisted.

"Then pull on down this driveway and we will show you and your wife that there ain't a house back here anymore."

Stewart clucked to Poppie as the young couple looked straight ahead. There before them was the foundation of a house and a crumbling chimney. Pieces of burnt wood lay rotting on the ground. A maple tree grew out of what was once the kitchen's floor.

Mary Grace gasped at what she saw. Stewart pulled the horse to a stop and ran over to the dilapidated barn. The hayrack was empty.

"Gentlemen," Stewart said as he stepped back, "There was half a bale of hay in this rack less than ten minutes ago. What happened to it?"

"There wasn't any hay in that rack ten minutes ago, or thirty years ago. You are confused," Mr. Henry said.

Mary Grace walked to the foundation of the burned-out house.

"Oh no, this can't be true. Stewart, come here quickly."

Stewart ran to his wife. The tone in her voice frightened him.

Mary Grace pointed to a pile of rotten clothes on a broken chair. She reached to touch them and they evaporated into the wind.

"Those were the clothes we slept in last night. Stewart, look there under the brush on the foundation. It's my note and the silver dollar. How is this possible?"

Mary Grace started to cry and ran to her husband. Stewart folded her in his arms and comforted her.

The men went to see the note and money for themselves. Richard Henry stepped onto the foundation and kicked wild grapevines out of his way. When he reached for the note and the money, a rabbit jumped from under a bush. Mary Grace screamed, the young man leaped backwards, and fell flat.

"Hurry up, Richard, get out of there," the father yelled.

"What's happening, I don't understand," Mary Grace cried.

None of the men had an explanation. They just looked at each other, confused and scared.

Stewart spoke, "There has to be an explanation."

"The only explanation is that you and your wife encountered the ghost of Vernon and Elenore Carpenter, who have been dead for fifty years. You knew a lot about them. I didn't want to admit it at first, but several things you mentioned about them were true. Vernon Carpenter was a master craftsman. He could make or build anything. Everyone said he had a knack for it. Going fishing was their favorite pastime. The night their house burned was a terrible time. The fire had gotten out of hand by the time the neighbors saw it. The Carpenters didn't have any chance to escape. I remember the night, not only for the fire, but the next day was my fifteenth birthday. Everyone was sad about losing their neighbors and I didn't get to celebrate."

The elderly man suddenly stopped talking.

"What's the matter, Papa?" Richard asked.

The old man shook his head in disbelief.

"What is it sir?" Stewart asked.

"Today is my sixty-fifth birthday! It's been exactly fifty years since the fire," Mr. Henry answered.

Mary Grace was close to fainting, so Stewart helped her into the buggy.

Mr. Henry and his son stood, staring at one another.

"Gentlemen, I don't know what has happened here, but I need to get my wife on to Harrodsburg. Please climb into the buggy so that we may be on our way."

"I'm ready to get out of here," Richard said.

They all got into the buggy. Stewart clucked to Poppie and they headed back to the main road. No one said anything; there wasn't anything to be said.

Stewart pulled Poppie to the side of the road and the men climbed out, right where they had left their tools.

"Gentlemen, nothing was solved by our return trip to the Carpenter's. In fact, more questions have been raised, questions that will never be answered. I'm not sure what my wife and I have experienced because there isn't any earthly way to explain it. So, at this time we shall take our leave from you. Perhaps sometime in the future, we will discuss this matter again. Now, good day to you gentlemen."

"Good day to you and your wife," the men said as they tilted their hats in the young couple's direction.

"How long before we reach Harrodsburg?" Mary Grace asked.

"No more than thirty minutes."

"Stewart, we will not mention this incident to Aunt Tolly."

"No, we won't tell her about it. We don't need to tell anyone about it. They wouldn't believe us anyway."

"Stewart?"

"Yes, Sweetheart, what is it?"

"When he head home, can we go back through Willisburg instead of coming back this way?"

"Mary Grace, from now on, I believe we will always come and go to Harrodsburg through Willisburg."

Two of a Kind

1910

Robert and Richard Phillips were identical twins, except for the color of their eye's. Robert's eyes were brown and Richard's were blue. They operated a grist mill on the Chaplain River. They inherited the property after their father died.

Robert was the businessman of the two brothers, shrewd, focused and reliable. He had secured new clients for the mill from as far away as Springfield. He had devised a better bagging system that kept more grain inside of the bag instead of on the floor.

Robert's main fault was his demeanor. He was short tempered and hot headed. Many men had felt his wrath, especially his brother Richard.

Richard was afraid of his brother. Being carefree and kindhearted, he tended to let his mind wander, and that made Robert mad. Richard enjoyed writing poetry and short stories. He sketched pictures of the mill and the flowing Chaplain River that ran through their farm. None of which his brother approved of.

On a beautiful spring day, Mr. Frank Brown stopped at the mill with his daughter, Jessa. She had been away at a finishing school in Chicago for the last three years. She had blossomed into a fine lady that Mr. Brown loved to show off.

"Mr. Robert Phillips, Mr. Richard Phillips, you both remember my daughter Jessa, don't you?"

"Of course, we do," Robert answered.

"How could we ever forget Miss Jessa? She was the best tree climber in the county," Richard said with a smile.

Robert and Richard were amazed at her beauty. They wondered how an ugly, skinny caterpillar of a girl could turn into such a beautiful butterfly. She floated on the air as she walked. Jessa possessed a certain flare that was impossible to deny.

Robert and Mr. Brown stood on the porch and talked about the price of the upcoming summers crops while Richard and Jessa walked over to the river. Robert looked over Mr. Brown's shoulder toward them just as Richard handed Jessa a bunch of spring daisies. Jessa excepted the flowers, brought them up to her face and smelled the freshness of spring. Robert noticed that Richard's gesture of flowers to Jessa seemed to make her happy. It made Robert mad.

Robert felt he was going to lose his composure. His neck stiffened up, his throat got tight. He excused himself from Mr. Brown and stepped into the mills office for a few minutes.

He felt the feeling of rage envelope his body. All of a sudden, he hated his brother for his free spirit, his artistic talents, his soothing voice. He hated everything about him.

Robert thought out the situation at hand. If his brother were out of the picture, he could court Miss Jessa as he pleased. But there wasn't any way to get his brother out of the picture, unless he killed him. It dawned on him he should talk to Mr. Brown about his daughter's personal situation. That would be the proper thing to do.

Robert straightened his shirt and returned to talk to Mr. Brown.

"Mr. Brown, has your daughter Jessa been promised in marriage to any one yet?"

"No, not yet, she's very independent. I don't believe she has any interest in marriage at this particular time. Besides, it would take a special kind of man to live with her."

Robert pictured himself as that special kind of man. Suddenly he felt very powerful.

"Mr. Brown, may I call on your daughter Jessa sometime in the future? With only good intentions, proper etiquette and the good manners that my Mama taught me."

"I don't know Mr. Phillips, she and her mother work out those type of things. Your best bet is to ask Jessa,"

"So, do I have your permission to ask her?"

"Yes, Robert, you have my permission to ask her."

As Robert and Mr. Brown walked around the mill, Richard and Jessa walked back toward them.

"Oh Father, look at the sketch Mr. Phillips drew of me, the likeness is striking, isn't it?"

"Yes, it is very nice Jessa. We better get going."

"Thank you for my drawing, Mr. Phillips."

"You are very welcome, Miss Brown, maybe I could sketch you again."

"I would like that Mr. Phillips."

"Please, call me Richard."

"Thank you, Richard. You may call be Jessa."

"Thank you, Miss Jessa."

"Goodbye, Richard," Jessa said as she climbed into her Father's wagon.

A strong pang of envy struck Robert when he heard Jessa's tone of voice. He realized Richard was winning over Jessa's attention with a silly drawing.

After the Browns left the mill Robert glared at Richard with an evil eye. Richard recognized the look and went into the house to avoid his brother's wrath.

Later that night, Robert hitched up the horses and drove to the Brown's farm on Horn Lane. When he knocked on the door, Mrs. Brown, Jessa's Mother, opened it.

"Hello Mrs. Brown, is your daughter Jessa here?"

"Yes, she is Mr. Phillips. She mentioned she had seen you today at your mill. Would you like to come inside?"

"No ma'am, may I speak to Jessa here on the front porch?"

"I will get her for you."

Robert sat down on the porch swing. His face darkened by the evening shadows.

"Hello Richard, how are you?"

"I am fine Miss Jessa. I've stopped by to see if you would honor me with your presence and accompany me to the church social this Saturday night?"

"I will have to ask my parents for permission to go."

"I spoke to your father today. He gave me permission to take you out."

"He did?"

"Yes, he did."

"Well, that being the case, I would like to attend the church social with you Richard."

"I will pick you up around six o'clock that evening."

"I look forward to it Richard. Maybe you could bring some of the poetry you have written and read it to me."

"Yes, maybe I will, until then Miss Jessa," Robert bowed his head to her.

Robert was pleased with himself. There wasn't any doubt that Jessa believed he was Richard, but he didn't care. She had accepted his invitation and he expected her to accompany him. After Jessa saw how important and successful he was, she would choose him over Richard. It seemed the perfect plan.

When Robert returned home, Richard was waiting to talk to him.

"Oh Robert, I think I am in love."

"In love with who?"

"With Jessa Brown! She is the sweetest, smartest, prettiest woman I have ever met. I plan on asking her to the church social. Since she was impressed with my drawings and my poetry, I think she will except my invitation. With a beautiful woman like her by my side, I would never ask for anything else."

"That's probably not going to work out for you brother."

"Why not?"

"Because, I have asked her to go with me to the church social."

"But I am the one who talked to her. I am the one she walked with."

"That may be so, but she is going to the social with me."

"You knew Jessa was interested in me. You didn't say three words to her today. What gave you the right to ask her out?"

"What gives me the right? I'll tell you what gives me the right, I saw Jessa at the same time you did. I just acted quicker and secured my place with her. Too bad brother."

"Robert? Was Jessa aware that it was you who asked her out, or did she think it was me?"

"She did mention something about bringing my poetry, and as you know, I don't write poetry," Robert replied with a sneer on his face.

"So, she did think you were me!"

"It is possible."

Richard was so mad he ran at Robert and knocked him off his feet.

"I should kill you now," Richard yelled at him.

"Go ahead brother, give it your best shot."

The brothers fought violently. They screamed and cursed and yelled as they wrestled around on the kitchen floor. They knocked over the furniture, and punched each other as hard as they could.

At one point Robert tried to cut Richard with a knife, but Richard knocked the knife from his hand. Robert picked up a broken chair leg and hit Richard's head with it. He continued to hit his brother until he fell to the floor in a thud. Richard's head was smashed in on the right side. His right eye was out of the socket. Blood ran out of his mouth and his ears. Most of his teeth were on the floor.

Robert sat down on a chair and looked around the room in a daze. His dead brother lay on the kitchen floor in front of him. His body faced upward, as his blue eyes stared blankly at the ceiling. Robert covered up Richard's face with a blanket.

At first Robert felt as if he had lost his mind. It seemed a part of himself had died too. He straightened up the room, broke up the rest of the chair and tossed it in the fireplace. The fire flamed up with a startling crack that produced a bluish flame.

Robert put Richard's body inside of a worn-out blanket and carried him into the woods. He buried the body in an orchard where the ground was soft and covered it over with moss.

As Robert walked back to the house, he devised a plan to explain his brother's absence. He decided he would tell people Richard took his inheritance and went to Europe to do his silly drawings. It was a believable story.

When Saturday night came, Robert arrived at Jessa's house at exactly six o'clock. His face was bruised and his knuckles were sore, but he had a good story to tell if anyone asked. He would say when he was realigning one of the grist stones, the wooden lever broke and slammed him into a wall.

Jessa was sitting on the front porch. "Good evening, Richard, how are you?"

"Good evening, Jessa, are you ready to go to the social?"

"Yes, sir, I am."

Robert helped her into his buggy. But he sensed she didn't need his help.

"Did you bring any poetry to read to me?"

"No, ma'am, I am Robert. Richard my brother is the poet."

"I would have sworn you said that you were Richard. I always had a hard time telling you two apart!"

"You must have misunderstood me. I assure you, I am Robert."

"Isn't this silly?" Jessa said. "I thought I was going out with Richard, and so did my parents. I guess it is easy to get confused when you are a twin. I will have to say I'm rather disappointed. No offense, but I always liked your brother better than you. Maybe I should just stay home."

Robert got upset from Jessa's. comments.

"Come on Miss Jessa. If you don't like me, you don't have to go out with me anymore. I think if you give me a chance, you'll see I'm a gentleman. Besides, Richard has left for an extended trip to Europe. I figured he had told you he was going when you met the other day."

"No, he didn't mention a word of it to me. I'll go with you tonight Robert but don't expect a second date with me."

Robert was so mad he couldn't see straight. He tried to make conversation with Jessa as they drove along, but his anger caused his words to slur.

When they arrived at Deep Creek Baptist Church a large crowd had already gathered in the front yard. Long tables filled with bowls and platters of food lined the sidewalk. Many people in the crowd waved at Jessa. They were excited to see her and several hurried over to the wagon.

Robert hitched the horses under a pin oak tree and helped Jessa down from the wagon.

"Robert, what happened to the side of your face?" Don't worry yourself about it, Miss Jessa. The wooden lever I used to realign one of the grist stones broke and threw me against the wall."

Preacher Carey walked up to Robert and said, "Robert, what happened to your face? You look like you've been in a fight. And where is Richard, isn't he coming?"

"No Preacher, he isn't coming. He left today for a trip to Europe to study art and different cultures. He's spending his inheritance money on something foolish, but I didn't say anything. It's his money."

"Richards gone to Europe? I didn't know Richard had plans to go abroad. It's hard to believe he wouldn't have mentioned it to us a hundred times."

"Well Preacher, the opportunity arose for him to secure a berth on a ship sailing out of New York City Tuesday afternoon, so he took it."

"It's not like Richard to not tell everything he knows. It seems peculiar, but then, sometimes your brother can be a little peculiar, no offense."

"No offense taken preacher. Oh, about my face being bruised, I had a fight with one of the grist stones, and the grist stone won," Robert explained jokingly.

"Yes, I can see you couldn't fight with a two-thousand-pound stone. I hope it doesn't get in the way of you courting."

"I don't expect it to. If you'll excuse me, I need to escort Miss Jessa through the food line now. Good day to you preacher."

"Good day Robert."

Robert and Jessa ate together, but few words were said.

On the ride home Robert tried to start a conversation, but Jessa's replies were very distant. Robert stopped the horses in front of the Brown's house and stepped down from the buggy. He extended his hand to help Jessa down, but she had gotten down by herself on the other side. Robert was taken aback by this act of independence. He followed her toward her front door.

"May I call on you again Miss Jessa?"

"No, Robert, you can't."

Jessa turned and walked into her house.

On his way home Robert's mind raced out of control. He slapped the horses with the reins and yelled curse words at them. He cursed his brother for being a poet and free spirit. He cursed Jessa for seeing the differences between them. He cursed himself for killing his brother.

Later that night Robert sat and looked at the fire in the fireplace. His mind wandered off into another world when he heard loud crazy laughter outside.

He called out, "Who's out there?"

No one answered him. The laughter came closer to the house. Robert looked out of the window, but he didn't see anyone. The laughter grew louder and louder. Robert closed his eyes tight and covered his ears, wishing the laughter would go away, but it didn't. When he opened his eyes, he saw his brother Richard's ghost standing right in front of him.

Richard's head was caved in on the right side and his right eyeball hung loose from its socket. Dried blood seeped from his ears, his nose and his mouth. Robert screamed out loud at the sight.

"What is the matter brother?" Richard's ghost asked in a groaning voice.

"What in God's name do you want?" Robert cried.

"I want you brother, what else could I want?"

"What do you mean?"

"We have been twins all of our lives. Sharing a bond that few will ever know. You killed me over a pretty woman. A pretty woman that wanted me instead of you. Have you written her a poem yet?"

Robert didn't answer. He went and hid behind a cabinet door.

"You cannot hide from me brother. We will always be twins so we must look alike. I am here to kill you so that you will always look like me."

Robert pleaded with his brother's spirit, "Please Richard, please don't kill me."

"I am afraid that I have to kill you, Robert."

Robert screamed out in pain, a scream that no one heard.

On Monday morning several farmers waited to grind their corn, but Robert had not opened the mill office. After a while, one of the farmers suggested that they check on Robert up at the house.

They knocked on the front door, but no one answered. One of the farmers opened the front door of the house and walked slowly. The room was in chaos. There were pieces of broken furniture thrown around everywhere. Food had been spilled on the floor and broken dishes lay everywhere.

The farmers noticed Robert's feet under the kitchen table. When they walked toward the body, they saw that Robert's face was covered over with a blanket. One of the farmers pulled the blanket back.

Robert's head was caved in on the right side and his eyeball hung loose from the socket. The other eye stared up at the ceiling. There was dried blood seeping out of his nose, his right ear and the side of his mouth. Most of his teeth were on the floor.

"Who would have done such a thing?" The farmers asked each other.

"He must have been the victim of a robbery."

"It's hard to believe a robber would bother to cover his face."

"He probably didn't want to look at Robert's eyes after he killed him. We had better go to town and get the sheriff, he'll know what to do."

As the men were leaving the house one of them said. "That is odd."

"What is it?"

"Look how fierce the fire is burning. I say Mr. Phillips has been dead for at least twenty-four hours. So, who kept the fire burning?"

"Maybe the robber was still here when we came, and ran away when he saw us."

"Yes, I suppose so."

"You go get the sheriff, we will wait here with the body."

The farmers who waited at the house talked among themselves.

"Richard Phillips left town on a trip to Europe last week. Wonder how we can find him to tell him about his brother's death?"

"I don't know how. I guess we'll have to wait until he finally comes home to tell him."

Robert was buried at Deep Creek Baptist Church, next to his parents. Several weeks later a man looking for ginseng found Richard's body in the woods. It was noticed that his injuries appeared very similar to Robert's. In fact, they were identical.

We've Got Company

1910

Great-Grandpa, William Harvey Leonard was standing on Main Street in Harrodsburg, talking to Robert Pullman about the upcoming tobacco market sale, when they heard men yelling.

They looked down Lexington Street and saw several men trying to move a loaded wagon off the railroad tracks. One man pulled on the horse's reins to move the wagon forward, but it wouldn't budge. Grandpa and Mr. Pullman hurried to the railroad tracks and attempted to help free the wagon.

There was a woman with a baby sitting in the wagon. The woman was crying and holding the baby tightly. She was wearing a red coat with an upturned collar. Her hair was twisted into a bun using a black celluloid comb.

A man, apparently the woman's husband, begged her to climb down but she was frozen with fear.

The men tried to get the wagon wheel unstuck from the tracks, but it wouldn't come loose. The load was too heavy for them to lift.

"How did the wagon wheel get stuck?" Grandpa asked.

"When the horse spooked at a dog, the wagon tilted sideways and caught the back wheel in the track," Bill Johnson told him.

"Well, we've got to get the wagon off the tracks. A train could come any minute now," Grandpa said.

The man pleaded with his wife to get out of the wagon, but she wouldn't move. He tried pulling her and the baby down to the ground, but she held on to the wagon seat.

He yelled and cursed at her while the other men continued to try and get the wheel out of the track. The wheel just wouldn't come loose.

The men unhitched the horse from its harness and tied the horse to a fence. They started to unload the wagon's cargo.

Grandpa Leonard talked to the woman in a soothing voice. He explained to her why she needed to get down from the wagon.

"Hand me your baby, then I can help you down."

The woman paid no attention to him, but continued to cry.

Suddenly everyone heard the train's whistle. Panic became chaos. The husband pulled his wife's body toward him, but she fought him. It was as if she had lost her mind.

From the other side of the wagon Grandpa Leonard tried to pry her hands from the seat. She would not let go.

The train was within a block of the scene. Richard Preston ran toward the train to get the train to stop, but it was moving too fast. The train's engineer saw Mr. Preston and hit the brakes. The screeching of the train's wheels on the steel rails was deafening.

The man screamed at his wife, but she didn't hear him. Grandpa Leonard jumped up on the wagon and pulled the woman with all his might. The train was there: it couldn't stop. The woman looked at Grandpa with fear in her eyes.

Robert Pulliam grabbed Grandpa Leonard away from the wagon only seconds before the train hit. Both men ended up on their backs on the ground. Two other men pulled the husband out of the way of the train just in time to save him.

When the train hit the wagon there was a loud scream and the sound of wood splintering. Dishes, furniture, and personal property scattered down the tracks and onto the street. The husband fainted.

The other men watched as the train dragged the wagon for another block and a half before coming to a stop.

Grandpa Leonard and three other men ran to where the train had stopped. The wagon, the woman, and the baby were crushed beyond recognition.

"What a terrible thing to happen! It's the worst accident I've ever seen," Grandpa said.

Half of Harrodsburg had arrived on the scene. The husband was carried to Dr. Wicklow's office for a sedative and the process of removing the bodies from under the train began.

Grandpa Leonard helped with the cleanup until all the body parts were collected and put into a wooden coffin.

He stopped by Dr. Wicklow's office on his way home. At least thirty people were standing in the front yard of the doctor's office.

"How's the man doing?" Grandpa asked.

"Dr. Wicklow gave him a sedative. He says the poor man is in shock."

"Do you know who the man is, or where he is from?"

"He told Dr. Wicklow his name was Daniel Ford. They think he might be from Bardstown, but they ain't sure."

"Well, it's a terrible thing. I'm going home," Grandpa told the crowd.

When Grandpa got to his house, he heard his daughter Pearlie crying.

"What's the matter with you Pearlie?"

"Mother thinks I'm lying and I'm not!"

"Lying about what?"

"About the woman I saw in the front parlor this afternoon."

Grandma Leonard came into the room and said, "Harve, you sure look tired tonight."

"It was an awful day in town. There was a terrible accident between the train and a wagon. A woman and her baby were killed!"

"Oh, no," Grandma and Pearlie said.

Grandpa sat at the kitchen table and said, "What were you crying about, Pearlie?"

"This afternoon, Mother and I felt a lot of cold air in the house. Mother sent me to check the windows and the front door. When I went into the hallway, I felt cold air coming from under the pocket doors going into the parlor.

I opened one door and thought a window must have fallen down. It was so cold in there. When I pulled back the curtains, the room was flooded with sunlight. I turned and saw a woman holding a baby sitting on the platform rocker."

"Who was it?" Grandpa asked.

"Pearlie didn't recognize her Harve. I think it was a shadow that Pearlie imagined was a person. You know she has trouble seeing from being cross eyed."

"I can see fine, Mother. Just because I'm cross eyed doesn't mean I can't see!"

"What did she say to you, Pearlie?" Grandpa asked.

"She didn't say anything. I asked her if she was here to visit with Mother, but she never answered. I told her I would go get Mother for her and I did."

"Harve, there wasn't anybody in the parlor when I went in there."

"I'm telling you Mother. I saw a woman and a baby."

"Pearlie, I know you think you saw somebody, but there wasn't anybody there. It was probably just a shadow."

"It wasn't a shadow, Mother. I saw a woman wearing a red coat with an upturned collar. Her hair was fixed up in a bun with a black celluloid comb.

The baby she was holding was wrapped in a blue blanket with the initials DNF stitched on it."

"That can't be possible!"

"What is it, Harve?"

"The woman who was killed in the buggy accident was wearing a red coat with an upturned collar. She had a black celluloid comb in her hair. The baby was wrapped in a blue blanket."

"Are you saying the woman and baby Pearlie saw in the parlor were the ghosts of the accident victims?"

"I know it sounds crazy, but the similarities are unbelievable."

"What were the initials you saw on the blanket Pearlie?"

"DNF. The initials were DNF. I'm certain of it."

"Before I left town, I heard the husband's name was Daniel Ford. That is two of the same initials."

Pearlie started to cry again.

"How is that possible Harve?"

"The only explanation is this: I was the last person on earth the poor woman and her baby saw. I'll never forget the look of fear I saw in her eyes. I was touching her coat only seconds before Robert Pullman pulled me to safety. Somehow her spirit passed through my house on her way to heaven. You said you both felt cold air in the house. Spirits travel through cold air, you both know that."

"I suppose you are right, Harve."

"Do you believe me now, Mother?" Pearlie asked.

"Yes, Pearlie. I do."

Kitty Kitty

Circa 1915

There was an old man named Mr. Curry who lived down on Johnson Pike. He was the most disagreeable man there ever was, cold, hateful and mean.

He would argue with you over what color the grass was. If you were dying of thirst, he wouldn't give you a drink of water out of his well.

In the summertime he would sit on his front porch and curse you when you passed. If he caught you fishing in his pond, he would have you arrested.

In the fall and winter, he sat at a window in the attic of his house. If you got to close too his pear tree he pounded on the window and yelled at you to get off his property.

The only thing Mr. Curry liked was his old cat Whiskers. The cat followed Mr. Curry everywhere.

One cold winter day a neighbor noticed Mr. Curry's body leaning against the attic's window of his house. The neighbor climbed the stairs and saw Mr. Curry's dead body sitting in an old rocking chair. On his lap was his cat Whiskers, who was dead too.

It seemed odd the cat died at the same time as Mr. Curry. Some people said the cat died from a broken heart. Others wondered if the cat died first, causing Mr. Curry to die of a broken heart.

Mr. Curry and Whiskers were buried on a hillside overlooking the farm's pond.

Several months later the farm was sold at auction. Everyone noticed all of the windows in the house were nailed shut. Someone commented Mr. Curry was probably trying to keep death out.

A family by the name of Winston bought the farm at the auction. The house was in deplorable condition from years of neglect.

The Winston's moved in and attempted to make the house livable. There were many things to do; The roof had to be patched to keep rain out, and the window frames had rotted and needed to be replaced.

The Winston's had three children; Thurman was twelve, Thomas was ten, and Elizabeth was nine.

Before they left their old farm at Duncan, Mrs. Turner Semones gave Elizabeth a kitten, a cute calico she named Daisy, after her favorite flower.

The first night in the house, Daisy scratched on the attic door and meowed.

"Make Daisy stop scratching on the door, Elizabeth," her Mother said, "She's driving me crazy."

Elizabeth shooed Daisy away, but in no time, Daisy returned and scratched on the door again.

"Elizabeth, if Daisy doesn't stop scratching on the door, she is going to have to live outside. I can't get any work done listening to her. Your Daddy would be mad if Daisy scratched the door frame up worse than it is now."

"Oh no, Mama, Daisy can't stay outside by herself; something might get her!"

"Well, if you can't get her to behave herself, she will be living outside. Do you hear me?"

"Yes, Mama, I hear you."

Everyone was tired and they all went to bed early. All of a sudden, they heard a creaking noise in the attic. Like someone was walking around up there. The children were scared; Mr. and Mrs. Winston were puzzled.

"What is that noise Daddy?" Thomas asked.

"It's just the wind, or maybe a raccoon. I'll see to it in the morning. Don't be worried."

The next morning Mr. Winston opened the attic door and climbed the stairs. Daisy Cat beat him to the top and went directly to an old rocking chair next to a window. The chair rocked back and forth as Daisy rubbed against it.

Mr. Winston realized the old chair rocking was the noise they had heard. He assumed the wind through the rotted windows caused the old chair to rock. He moved the old rocking chair over to the middle of the attic. When he went back downstairs, he decided to nail the attic door shut for now.

All day Daisy scratched and meowed at the attic door.

"Make Daisy stop scratching the door, Elizabeth," Mrs. Winston insisted.

Elizabeth tried to keep Daisy away from the door. By playing with her, picking her up and holding her. As soon as Elizabeth put Daisy down, she would run back and started scratching again.

"That's enough Elizabeth; Daisy needs to live outside."

"No, Mama, please, give her one more chance. I'll keep her away from the door."

"One more chance; that's all she gets."

Elizabeth watched Daisy every minute. If the cat started toward the attic door, Elizabeth would make a loud noise or throw a paper wad. Daisy changed directions, but her mind stayed focused on the attic door.

All that day Daisy scratched on the door. She meowed, jumped on it, and walked back and forth rubbing her body against it. She grabbed at the doorknob with her paws and purred loudly.

"That's it. I'm sorry Elizabeth, but Daisy needs to live outside."

"Please, Mama, please don't put her out. If something happens to her my heart will be broken."

"Elizabeth, Daisy has become a nuisance messing with that door all the time. It makes me nervous. She'll be fine. Most cats live outside anyway."

"Alright, Mama, but if Daisy gets hurt, I'm blaming you and Daddy for my broken heart."

Elizabeth carried Daisy outside, and sat her on the front porch swing, where Daisy stretched, curled up and went to sleep.

Elizabeth checked every fifteen minutes. She sighed with relief when she saw Daisy hadn't moved.

Around suppertime Elizabeth looked for Daisy, but she wasn't on the swing or the front porch. She wasn't under the bushes or up in the trees. Elizabeth called and called for Daisy, but Daisy never came.

"Mama, I can't find Daisy. I've looked everywhere!"

"She'll be all right. It's time for supper, go call your brothers."

"Yes, ma'am."

The family had started eating, when they heard a scratching on the other side of the attic door.

"What in the world is that?" Thomas asked.

"I don't know, maybe just the wind," Mr. Winston said.

"How can the wind make a scratching noise?" Elizabeth asked.

The scratching become louder. The whole family looked at the attic door and saw the doorknob turning back and forth.

"There must be a ghost up there!" Thurmond screamed.

Elizabeth hid her face in her Mother's lap.

"There isn't any ghost; it's probably a bird," Mr. Winston assured his family.

The door continued to rattle and the doorknob turned back and forth. The children were scared and wouldn't eat. Thomas and Elizabeth started to cry.

"Children, there isn't anything for you to be afraid of. Your Daddy told you it is probably the wind or a bird in the attic. There aren't any ghosts in this house."

"Are you sure Mother?" Thurmond asked.

"Yes, Son, I am sure."

After supper, Elizabeth went outside to look for Daisy. She called and called but Daisy never came.

"Mama, I still can't find Daisy, something has happened to her."

"No, it hasn't, Daisy's probably in the barn. She probably made herself a bed in here She will be fine. I bet Daisy will be on the front porch in the morning."

"Really, Mama? Do you really think so?"

"Yes, Elizabeth, I really do."

As soon as they went to bed, they heard the same noise in the attic they had heard the previous night.

"Daddy, there is that noise again," Thurmond yelled.

"It's just the wind blowing. Don't worry, go to sleep."

Mr. Winston told his wife, "I thought the noise was from an old rocking chair sitting next to a window. I moved it to an inside wall. I don't understand how it could be rocking now. The wind can't be hitting it. I'll check in the morning when I get back from town."

Elizabeth couldn't sleep. She kept hearing noises.

At sun up she went to look for Daisy. She looked all over the yard, and checked every nook in the barn, but Daisy wasn't anywhere. Tears ran down Elizabeth's face as she walked back to the house.

Something in the attic window caught her attention. When she looked up she saw Daisy sitting in the attic window, meowing at her.

"Mama, Mama, I found Daisy! I found Daisy!"

"Where did you find her?"

"She's sitting in the attic window, meowing at me. We have to get her out of there right now! She might be hurt!"

"How in the world did that cat get up into the attic? Did you open the door for her?"

"No, Mama, I didn't, but that is where she is. Hurry, let's go."

"We'll have to wait for your Daddy to come. I don't want to go up to the dirty attic."

"How long before Daddy is coming home?"

"He should be back in about an hour."

"I'm going to wait for Daddy."

Elizabeth looked up, but Daisy wasn't there.

She called, "Daisy, Daisy, come back to the window."

Daisy returned to the windowsill, her body arched.

"Don't worry Daisy. Daddy will get you out when he gets home."

Elizabeth sat below the window, talking to Daisy.

Finally, her Daddy walked up the driveway.

"Oh, Daddy, Daisy is locked in the attic."

"How did that cat get into the attic?"

"I don't know, but she is up there. Look, don't you see her in the window?"

"Yes, I see her. I guess we know who the ghost was in the attic last night."

Elizabeth smiled and said, "Yes Daddy, I suppose we do."

"Mama, Daddy is home. He's going to get Daisy for me."

"I'm glad Elizabeth."

Mr. Winston got the hammer to remove the nail from the attic door, but the nail was gone.

"Who took the nail out of the door?"

"None of us took the nail out. Maybe it fell out."

When Mr. Winston opened the door, Daisy ran down the stairs and jumped right into Elizabeth's open arms and purred loudly.

"I hate to look in that attic; I imagine it is a mess," Mrs. Winston told her husband.

"It doesn't look too bad, just dusty," he replied. "What I want to know is how Daisy got up there. Maybe there's hole in the roof or a window that's broken. Let's go look."

Mr. and Mrs. Winston started up the attic stairs. The cat ran up in front of them.

"Daisy, come back!" Elizabeth cried.

"We'll get her, Elizabeth. Calm down."

Mr. Winston looked around the attic for a hole, but he didn't see any sunlight coming in.

"Oh, my Lord!" Mrs. Winston exclaimed.

"What is it?"

"What is it, Mama?" Elizabeth called from the bottom of the stairs.

Mrs. Winston pointed to the rocking chair. It was back over next to the window rocking on its own. Daisy walked back and forth beside of it, arching her back and tail, and lowering her head as if rubbing on someone's shoes.

The Winston's watched, amazed as the chair continued to rock.

"Mama? Can I come up there?"

"No, Elizabeth. You wait there."

Mr. and Mrs. Winston looked at each other, not understanding what they were witnessing, but Daisy wasn't confused. She seemed to be perfectly content as she walked around the rocking chair and purred loudly.

The Winston's felt afraid. Something strange was happening and they didn't want their children to know about it. Mrs. Winston called Daisy, and the cat responded immediately and ran down the steps in front of them.

Thurman and Thomas were with Elizabeth in the kitchen when their Mother came in.

"What was up in the attic, Mama?" the children asked.

"Nothing but a few wasps and a lot of hot air. Some day we might clean it up and have an extra room."

Mr. Winston descended and closed the door behind him. He nailed the door shut again.

"May we go up to the attic, Daddy?" Thomas asked.

"Not today, Son."

"Why not, Daddy?"

"Because you don't need to go up there, that's why." Mr. Winston answered sternly.

"Why are you nailing the door shut Daddy?"

"I don't want the wind to blow it open and scatter all of the dust and dirt down the stairs and into the house, especially after your Mother has worked so hard to get the house clean."

The answer seemed to satisfy the children.

For the third night they heard the noise in the attic. The next morning Daisy started scratching on the door again.

"Elizabeth, put Daisy outside, she can come in at night."

Elizabeth did as she was told.

Less than an hour later, as she was hanging wet clothes on the line, Mrs. Winston saw Daisy in the attic window.

"That darn cat. How did she get up there? One of the children must have let her in."

"Daisy is in the attic again. One of the children took the nail out of the door and let her in, I guess," she told her husband.

Mr. Winston called his children into the kitchen.

"Which one of you took the nail out of the door?"

"We didn't take the nail out Daddy," they all answered.

"Then how did the cat get back up there?"

"We don't know Daddy."

Mr. Winston went back up the attic stairs to get the cat. The rocking chair was rocking and Daisy was purring to beat the band.

Mr. Winston nailed the door shut again as his children watched. When he had completed the job, he sent his children to the barn to gather eggs.

He said to his wife, "I'm going to talk to Father French. Maybe he can shed some light on this situation. Something's going on I don't understand."

"I sure hope Father can help us. I've never seen such a thing," Mrs. Winston said with a shiver.

Mr. Winston walked to Saint Nicholas Catholic Church. Luckily, Father French was there. As he told the priest the unbelievable story, Father French listened intently.

"I believe I understand this situation."

"You do? Please Father, explain it to me."

"Your family moved into Mr. Curry's house. It was a known fact Mr. Curry said he would never leave the farm. He nailed the windows closed to keep death from coming to get him. I believe that instead of keeping death away from him, it actually trapped Mr. Curry's spirit in the house. There wasn't anyway for his spirit to leave and go to Heaven. The attic was as far as he could get."

"So, what are you saying we should do, Father? If his spirit is trapped in the attic?"

"You must open the window in the attic so his soul can escape the clutches of this world."

"Do you think that will put an end to this situation?"

"Yes, Mr. Winston, I do."

"Oh, thank you, Father, I surely appreciate it."

"Mr. Winston?"

"Yes, Father?"

"The only friend Mr. Curry had was his old cat, Whiskers. Did you know he kept a cat in the house?"

"No Father, I didn't know that."

"When they found Mr. Curry dead, he was sitting in an old rocking chair in the attic. Whiskers the cat was dead on his lap. The local men who buried Mr. Curry buried Whiskers with him. Oh, and one more thing before you go Mr. Winston."

"What is it Father?"

"Some folks around here believe that cats can see ghosts. Maybe your daughter's cat saw the ghost of Mr. Curry."

"Maybe it did Father French, thank you, again."

Mrs. Winston was waiting for her husband on the front porch.

"What did Father French tell you?" she asked.

"Where are the children?" he asked.

"I sent them over to Mrs. Taylor's house with a loaf of bread. They won't be back for a while."

"Then we should do what Father French told me to do, while they are gone."

"What did Father French say?"

"Follow me and I will show you."

The nail was missing from the door once again. They both climbed the stairs slowly. Daisy was waiting for them at the top.

"I'm afraid!" Mrs. Winston said.

"Don't be afraid; it will be all right," Mr. Winston assured her.

Daisy ran over to the chair, that was rocking again.

Mr. Winston removed the nails that held the window closed, and raised the window.

The rocking chair leaned forward and stayed in that position for several seconds.

The Winston's couldn't believe what they were seeing.

Then, as if someone had stood up from the chair, it rocked back and forth, then stopped.

Daisy's eyes followed something invisible toward the open window. She ran to the window, and jumped to the sill. She meowed loudly, like a kitten crying for its mother.

Mrs. Winston picked Daisy up and held her tight.

"Should I close the window?" Mr. Winston asked.

"No, leave it open for a while, just in case anything else needs to leave for Heaven, or someplace else."

"Look there on the floor."

Lying beside the chair were three nails.

The children returned from Mrs. Taylor's house around six o'clock. Mrs. Winston had cooked a big pot of pinto beans and fried cornbread for supper. Daisy slept quietly on the sofa as the family ate.

Nothing was mentioned about the attic for several days. No one heard any noises.

One day, while sitting in the kitchen with her Mother, Elizabeth asked, "Mama? Have you and Daddy noticed that Daisy hasn't been scratching on the attic door lately?"

"Now that you mention it Elizabeth, she hasn't been. Daisy has been a good girl."

"You know, Mama, it's almost like Daisy lost interest in going up there. It's like she doesn't have any reason to go to the attic. Wonder why?"

"I guess it's just as you said, Elizabeth; she doesn't have any reason to go up there anymore."

Listen, Hear the Baby?

1915

Many years ago, down on the Chaplain River, there lived a couple and their baby son. Married for three years, the baby was their first child.

The man had always been mean to his wife. He beat her when he was drunk, he beat her when he was sober. There didn't seem to have to be a particular reason, he beat her all the time. Everyone knew about it but in those days, people minded their own business.

The young woman could hardly stand the sight of her husband, or the feel from the touch of his hand, let alone the sound of his voice. She married him thinking he would sober up and become the man she had dreamed of. He had good manners and talked sweet the night he asked her Daddy for her hand in marriage. She was afraid of him in some ways, but her family convinced her she might end up an old maid, being she was twenty-four years old. They told her she should marry this man, and thank her lucky stars that anyone would want to marry her in the first place. So, she married him.

She soon learned what an evil soul he possessed. Not only did he beat her, he called her awful names, blamed her for everything that went wrong, and deprived her of food. Her life was more than miserable.

She went to talk to her Daddy and begged him to let her come home. She explained to him how mean and hateful her husband was to her. But her Daddy's heart was cold.

He told her, "Maybe if you were a better wife, he would be a better husband. Now go on girl, get back home to your husband and act like you've got some sense."

Now that the baby had come at least she had some joy in her life. She spoke to her son softly. The baby looked up at her, cooing and suckling. He smiled and yawned and cried. All of her attention and love were focused entirely on her son. Everything he did was wonderful to her.

On into winter it was a terrible cold night with the temperature well below zero. The wind blew in from the north, swirling the snow on the ground straight up, turning it into an icy blizzard. The last pieces of wood her husband had chopped that morning had burned down to embers in the fireplace. It was barely warmer in their cabin than it was outside, so she held her son close to her body. He cried, then coughed. She was afraid he might be getting pneumonia.

She wrapped the baby in another blanket and lay down next to him on the bed. The poor woman figured her body's heat would help keep her son warm. There weren't any other options.

Several hours later her husband came home. He pushed the front door wide open as he entered the house. He let the howl of the wind and large snowflakes follow him inside.

"Hurry, shut the door," she said to him, "I don't want the baby to be any colder than he is now."

"Oh, that's too damn bad. I'll shut the door when I damn well please. Besides, it stinks in here, a little fresh air will clear it out," he said as he smirked in her direction.

"Please, the baby is coughing and crying. I don't want him to get sicker, I'm trying to keep him warm," she pleaded.

"If you are so damn cold, why didn't you put more wood on the fire? You stupid bitch. Those hogs in the lot out there are smarter than you."

"I've used all the wood you cut this morning, there's none left."

"Well, you'll just have to wait until the morning, because I'm not cutting any firewood tonight. Besides, any idiot knows you save most of the wood for the night. But you are a stupid idiot, I guess that explains that, doesn't it?"

"Why are you so mean to me?"

"Because you are lazy, ugly, and stupid."

"Why did you marry me if you found me so obnoxious?"

"I was drunk when your Daddy offered you up to me for marriage. He said he would sweeten the pot with five hogs and three milk cows. I needed someone to cook and wash my clothes. That's why I married you. I was drunk when we got married, and due to your stupidity, I've stayed drunk ever since."

She began to cry. Everything in her life was out of her control and it was impossible for her to see any changes in the future. She lay down beside her son as he continued to cry and cough.

"Where's my supper at woman. Get it for me now."

"There's collard greens and cornbread on the stove."

"Greens again, can't you cook anything but greens?"

"That's all I had to cook tonight."

He ate the entire bowl of collard greens and washed them down with swigs of cheap whiskey. When he finished eating, he slung the empty bowl to the floor with his arm. Vinegar ran across the table, dripping to the floor.

"Clean up this mess before you go to sleep," he told her, burping out loud.

She cleaned up his mess just like she always did. She couldn't take the chance of making him mad at her because her body was still bruised and sore from the last beating.

When he went to bed he pulled the blanket off the baby, covering himself with it instead.

"We need to share the blankets, the baby and I are cold."

"I'm cold too. If you had saved some wood for tonight, we wouldn't be having this problem, would we? Besides, I'm the money earner around here, it's more important for me to stay warm and healthy then it is for you. Without me woman, you ain't got a pot to pee in."

The poor woman climbed into bed, holding her son next to her. He felt cool to her touch, so she took off her tattered sweater and wrapped it around his body. He cried, then coughed up bloody phlegm.

"Can't you keep that baby quiet, I can't get no sleep."

"I'm doing all I can do for him. He's sick, do you hear me, he's sick."

"Yeah, I believe he's sick, being he's part yours he's bound to be sickly. I tell you what woman, now that this baby is here, I don't care if you are here or not. If you fell down a well, I'd leave you there. If the cattle ran you over in the field, I would plow you up under the dirt. If you were dying of thirst, I wouldn't give you a swig of water. The way I look at it, it would be good riddance to have you gone. Your stupid and ugly, you can't cook nothing fit to eat. The only reason I've kept you around for as long as I have was to get myself a son, I've got one now, and I don't give a damn about you."

She started to cry, holding her baby closer to her. The tears dripped off her face onto her sons face and ran down his cheeks.

Her husband fell asleep in no time at all. Cheap whiskey numbs your senses. She was exhausted too, but she couldn't go to sleep. She was afraid to sleep. What if the baby needed her during the night? She wouldn't hear him over her husband's snoring.

All of a sudden it felt like her brain was on fire. As if the top of her head would explode. Her vision was cloudy and she couldn't catch her breath. The cabin seemed to be swirling around in circles. It made her dizzy and sick to her stomach. She grabbed the baby and walked outside, leaving the cabins front door wide open. Her husband snores were as loud as a steam engine barreling down the railroad tracks, so he didn't hear a sound. He wasn't even fazed by the cold air rushing in since the liquor in his body was keeping him warm.

The poor woman cried more as she walked down the road holding her son tightly in her arms. Her flannel night gown drug the frozen ground behind her as she walked along. Tears were freezing to her face now, but she continued away from the house. Not knowing where she was going, or why.

The baby 's cough sounded deeper in his chest to her now. His cry seemed weaker too. Her son was sick and she needed to find someone to help her with him. But there wasn't anyone within a mile of where she was.

When she reached the iron bridge on Deep Creek Road she stopped. The metal bridge was frozen solid. Icicles hung down from the bridge's suspensions, reflecting the movement of the water in the river below. She looked at her son, then down into the cold dark water of the Chaplain River.

As if she were a woman possessed, she tossed her baby into the river. She heard the splash, then the sound of the baby crying. She couldn't think straight. What was she doing here? Why was she on this bridge in the middle of the night? She must be losing her mind she thought to herself.

As if awakened from a dream, reality returned to her. "Oh, my God, what have I done? Hold on my dear son, I'm coming to get you."

She jumped over the bridges railing, and fell into the river.

The bodies were discovered two days later, one mile downstream. They were found together, floating between the limbs of a downed oak tree.

* * * *

Circa-1950

Over the years it was said if you drove over the bridge on Deep Creek Road and killed your car's engine, you would hear a baby crying. One night, my parents and aunt and uncle went down to the bridge to look for the ghosts. They stopped the car right in the middle of the bridge and turned off the engine. They got out of the car and walked over to the bridges railing. They looked down into the darkened waters of the Chaplain River. Everything was very quiet as they listened intently for a baby's cry.

"I think I hear something, listen real close."

"Ssshhhh, listen, I tell you I hear something too."

All of a sudden, everyone else heard it too. It was a baby crying.

"Let's get out of here, I don't want to see a dead baby or his dead mother," My Aunt said.

Uncle Owen spoke up, "That's not a baby crying, it's a night hawk calling. I've heard them all my life."

"I've heard night hawks all my life too Owen, but I'm telling you that isn't a night hawk. It may not be a baby crying, but it's not a night hawk," Daddy told him.

There was a rustling in the bushes beside the river and they all looked in that direction. A white mist was rising up from the river, next to the bank. Without saying a word, they ran back to the car. As they drove away my Mother looked back towards the bridge. Standing in the middle of the bridge was a woman holding a baby. She was soaking wet and crying.

Mama screamed out, "I just saw the ghost of that poor woman holding her baby. She was standing in the middle of the road behind us."

No one questioned Mama about what she saw. They were too scared to look back to see for themselves. Daddy shifted the car into second gear, stepped on the gas and got the heck out of there. They never went back there again.

Other people claimed to see the ghost of a woman on the bridge over the next thirty years. I went with friends to the bridge in the 1990's, but we didn't hear or see anything. Maybe spirits grow weaker as years pass us by.

Sparks A Flying

1920

My Grandmother Henry's brother's name was Charles McCrystal, but people called Bud. He was a good fellow; He wouldn't rob you or tell you a lie. Bud respected his family, his church and his God. He never coveted his neighbor's wives, or took the Lord's name in vain. He toiled in the rocky fields of their farm, never complaining of work that always lay ahead of him.

But when Saturday night came, Bud would cut loose. He would ride his horse, Piper, into Harrodsburg and drink his fill of liquor. In fact, Bud had his trip planned out before he left his house. He would warm Piper in a slow canter, then bring him to a walk when they reached Mr. Willie Black's house, because Willie was always good for a swig or two of moonshine.

Bud would talk with Mr. Black for awhile about farming and the news of the county, managing to bring up his thirst for a little "shine," and Mr. Black always obliged. Bud knew he had time to reach town and the Saturday night activities, so after a few minutes he thanked Mr. Black for his hospitality, tilted his hat, and rode Piper on toward town.

Bud and Piper's next stop would be at Mrs. Bush Harvey's house. A well-known bootlegger for many years, she sat on her porch looking for customers regardless of the weather.

"Good afternoon Mrs. Harvey," Bud would say as he rode into her yard.

"Well, I swear, there's that good looking Bud McCrystal. Riding his fancy horse into my yard. Don't let your horse poop in my yard. My place has to make a good impression on my customers."

"I'll hitch him over here. Will that do?"

"Yes, that will do."

Bud hitched the horse in the shade at least thirty feet away from the house.

"How have you been this week, Mrs. Harvey?"

"I've been fair," she answered. "Come on up here on the porch Bud, so that I can see those blue eyes of yours."

Bud sat down on the front steps, looked up at Mrs. Harvey with those pretty blue eyes and said, "Got anything to drink tonight?"

"Are you talking about buying my whiskey? Or just drinking my whiskey?"

"Maybe a little of both, I would appreciate a short swig. Then on my way home from town tonight I'll stop by here and buy some from you."

"You won't have any money left by the time you come back from town," Mrs. Harvey protested.

"Yes, I will," Bud said as he smiled at Mrs. Harvey.

"I can't resist those eyes of yours Bud. Sit there, I'll get the jug."

Bud leaned back on the steps and under his breath he said, "Thank you God, for my blue eyes."

Mrs. Harvey brought a stone jug, uncorked it, and handed it to Bud. He accepted it, smiling up at her from his seat.

"Remember, a short swig is all you are getting."

Bud raised the jug to his mouth and the smell of moonshine caused him to shiver so he took a big swig, then another.

"Hold on there, Bud, I said one short swig."

He wiped his mouth with his shirtsleeve and put the cork back into the stone jug, and handed it back to her.

"Thank you, Mrs. Harvey. That hit the spot. Your moonshine is the best in the county, maybe in the whole state. It's awful smooth."

"I pride myself on making moonshine. I've got a secret ingredient, but I ain't going to tell you what it is. Go on and get out of here, Bud McCrystal. You better stop here on your way home and buy some shine from me. You already drank fifty cents worth."

"If you say so," Bud replied.

When he stood up to leave, the moonshine rushed to his head.

"Oh, it's going to be a fine night tonight, a fine night," he thought to himself.

"I'm thanking you for that good swig Mrs. Harvey. I'll see you on my way home. Being it's a full moon tonight, you should be able to see Piper and me coming down the road."

"I'll be watching for you my blue-eyed boy."

Bud climbed on Piper and clucked to him. The horse responded by raising his head high, and trotted down the road.

Bud rode up the lane leading to Elmer Jenkins' farm but no one was home. "Too bad," Bud thought to himself. "Elmer always has a little liquor hidden in his shed."

"Oh, well, Piper, let's go on to town."

They passed Harrodsburg's Water Works building on the banks of Salt River where Bud noticed several people were fishing. He turned Piper to the right, and walked him down the steep banks of the river.

"Look who's coming, it's Bud, my buddy, McCrystal," Jack Warner called.

Jack was fishing with Carl McGlone and Wooly Huff.

"Hey fellows, are you catching anything?" Bud asked.

"We've been here for two hours and ain't caught nothing," Carl answered.

"I don't think these worms are any good."

"There's something wrong with them," Wooly added.

Bud started laughing and said, "I can tell you why the fish ain't biting today."

"Oh, you can, can you, Mr. Smarty Pants?" Jack asked.

"As a matter of fact, I can. Do you not know that when the cows lay down in the field, the fish won't bite?"

"I have heard that saying, now that you mention it."

"So have I," Wooly and Jack said simultaneously.

"Are the cows laying down today, Bud?"

"I noticed all of Elmer Jenkins cows were down, chewing their cuds."

"Well, I'll be! Of all days we pick to go fishing. We might as well head back to town boys. Hey, Bud, can we ride with you on your horse?"

"All three of you? I don't think so. Unless you've got something to pay for your ride."

"We ain't got any money, Bud."

"I'm not talking about money. I'm talking about something to drink."

"We ain't got none of that either."

Bud knew they were telling the truth since all three of the men were sober.

"I've got some tobacco that's been soaked in whiskey at my house in town. I'll roll you a cigarette made from it, if you'll give me a ride to town," Jack told Bud.

"It's a deal, Jack. Jump on up here on Piper's back."

Jack hopped right up.

"What about us?" Carl and Wooly asked.

"See you in town, boys," Bud called while reeling Piper's head around to go up the steep bank. The two men and the horse went on their way.

Bud kept Piper in a slow trot, being he was carrying two men. Piper was Bud's most prized possession, so taking care of him was a high priority.

Bud slowed Piper down to a walk when they reached the city limits. Piper was sweating when they reached Jack Warner's house. Bud stopped Piper at the picket fence and Jack scooted down.

"Wait here, Bud. I'll get the cigarette for you."

"I'm not going anywhere until you get back Jack."

After only a few minutes, Jack returned and handed Bud the cigarette.

"I rolled you a big one, Bud."

"Thanks, Jack, you got a match?"

"Here, I brought one. I figured you would want to light it up."

"Sure do."

Jack struck the match and lit the end of the cigarette for Bud and he drew the smoke into his mouth.

"Got a sweet taste to it," Bud remarked.

"It was soaked in real good whiskey. I get dizzy if I smoke too much."

"Oh, good," Bud said, "I like being dizzy; I think it's fun. Maybe I'll see you downtown tonight, Jack."

Main Street was hopping when Bud and Piper arrived. Bud hitched the horse in the shade of a tree in the courthouse yard. He straightened his hair and smoothed his clothes. He was still smoking the whiskey-soaked cigarette as he walked down the hill.

"I'm getting a good buzz from this," Bud said to himself.

Harrodsburg had two poolrooms-one for the city boys and one for the county boys. Seemed if the two groups got together they wanted to fight, especially if they had been drinking. More than one knife had been drawn on Main Street, and the sound of gunfire had echoed between the buildings.

Bud swaggered into the Mercer County Poolroom and found a seat at the bar. The card tables were full of Rook players. Bud ordered a double shot of whiskey and the bartender obliged.

"That's twenty-five cents."

Bud slugged the drink. "Give me another one bartender."

"You haven't paid for this one yet."

"Here's a fifty-cent piece. Now fill up my glass."

Bud took his drink to one of the pool tables, thinking, "Oh, yeah, I'm getting drunk. I like it. Who wants to play a game of pool for money?"

Several people looked his way, but no one took his offer. So, he finished his drink in one big swallow and left. His balance was a little off, but he was o.k.

Bud saw Miss Jane Sparrow ahead of him, so he hurried to catch up with her.

"Miss Sparrow, how are you today?"

"Oh, Mr. McCrystal, so nice to see you."

"It's nice to see you, too. Would you let me buy your supper at The Harrod Hotel, Miss Sparrow?"

"That's a lovely idea, Mr. McCrystal, but I can't tonight. My mother invited company to our house for supper and she's expecting me to be there. I can't disappoint her. Maybe another time, Mr. McCrystal."

"Of course! Another time would be wonderful."

"Mr. McCrystal, are you coming to the county fair next week?"

"I was planning on it."

"Maybe I'll see you there."

"I hope so. And Miss Sparrow, please call me Bud."

"That seems too informal to me."

"Call me Charles then."

"All right, I'll call you Charles. See you next week Charles."

"See you then Miss Sparrow."

"Oh, Charles?"

"Yes, Miss Sparrow?"

"You may call me Jane."

"Thank you very much Jane."

Bud tipped his hat and smiled with his blue eyes sparkling.

He noticed there was a lot of commotion down the street at the Harrodsburg Pool Room. It sounded like a fight fixing to brew out the front door at any second, so he waited across the street to see what was going to happen. The fighters erupted onto the sidewalk with fists flying and legs kicking and lots of loud cursing. As always, the crowd urged the fighters on. Bud couldn't tell who the fighters were, but he recognized many in the crowd.

"Go on where you belong," someone said.

A man staggered from the crowd and fell in the street. Another man helped him up.

"We don't want to ever see you two around here again. If we do, you won't be able to walk home. Go on, get."

It was Kenneth Jones talking, the owner of the Poolroom.

"Now that we've got rid of those thieves, a free drink for everyone."

The crowd cheered. Bud couldn't turn down a free drink, even if it was inside the city pool room. No one would notice him. He would get a free drink, then slip out.

Mr. Jones filled shot glasses with cheap whiskey and lined the glasses along the bar. Bud reached for a glass but a hand grabbed his hand.

"What are you doing in here country boy? This pool room is for the city boys. Not you country bumpkins."

Bud looked up to see that Steven Macinaw had ahold of his hand.

"You are not the owner here," Bud told him.

"I'm not the owner, but the owner doesn't want your type in here."

"Look, Macinaw, I'm not looking for a fight, just a free drink of whiskey. Leave me alone."

Macinaw let go. Bud grabbed a shot glass filled with whiskey and drank it in one gulp.

"Hey, bartender, give me another shot," Bud called.

"You don't need another one, McCrystal. You're weaving like a loom now. Go on back to the other pool room," Mr. Jones warned.

"Just one more for the road," Bud pleaded.

"Didn't you hear what Kenneth told you, boy?" Macinaw asked.

"I don't see that it's any of your business, Macinaw," Bud said.

"I'm making it my business. Go on and get your Irish Catholic ass out of here."

"Don't you insult my heritage or religion, Macinaw. I won't stand for that."

"You won't be standing anything if you don't make tracks."

"Are you threatening me, Macinaw?"

"I'm telling you how it is."

"All right boys, break it up. We've had enough arguing for one day," Mr. Jones said.

"I'm going, but we will finish this some other time, Macinaw."

"Suits me just fine, McCrystal."

Bud walked back to the Mercer County pool room where he was welcome. Some of his friends were playing pool, so he got a double shot and joined them.

"Where you been, Bud?" Billy Burton asked.

"I've been down to the city poolroom."

"What were you doing there?"

"Getting a free drink."

"They were giving away free drinks?"

"Yep, they sure were."

"How come?"

"They were celebrating from running two men out of town."

"Who were the men?"

"I don't know, but that idiot Macinaw was giving me a hard time. Talking bad about my heritage and religion. I didn't like it a bit. One of these days I'm going to lock horns with him. He's got it coming."

"Macinaw is quick to draw a knife, even quicker to draw a gun. I'd leave him alone if I were you Bud," Billy Horn said.

"He's all talk and no action," Bud told Billy and the other men.

"Nevertheless, you've had too much to drink to be fighting with Macinaw."

"I'm not drunk."

"You're not drunk? You look drunk. How many fingers am I holding up?"

"Three."

"I'm only holding up two fingers. You are drunk, Bud. You need to settle down before you get yourself in trouble."

"I suppose you're right. I'm going to go sit at the bar and I'll talk to you fellows later."

Bud had two more shots of whiskey and noticed it had gotten dark. He didn't care; it made no difference to him.

Around nine o'clock, Nat Browning came running into the poolroom yelling at the top of his lungs.

"Bud, Bud, come quick, Macinaw is whipping your horse."

"What?"

"Macinaw is out there whipping your horse."

"He'd better not be," Bud said as he stumbled outside.

In the distance, Bud could see Macinaw holding a bullwhip. He yelled.

"Leave my horse alone you son of a bitch."

Macinaw didn't pay any attention. He smacked the horse's withers with the whip, causing Piper to neigh loudly and kick-out his hind legs.

Bud jumped on Macinaw's back, and grabbed the whip out of his hand.

"Don't you ever lay a hand on my horse again, or I'll kill you."

Bud raised the whip, and slashed it across Macinaw's shoulder.

Bud went to Piper, soothing him with his voice.

"You damn cheating lying Irishman."

Bud turned, and saw that Macinaw had a gun pointed at him. He pulled the trigger.

"I'm shot!" Bud cried out.

A crowd headed toward him.

"I'm shot in my shoulder! Someone go get Doctor Bailey."

"Doctor Bailey ain't in town. He went over to Lancaster to visit his sister. He won't be back until Monday."

"Help me on my horse. Mama can doctor me when I get home."

"You're hurt bad, Bud. You are losing a lot of blood. You better stay in town."

"No, I'm going home."

The men helped Bud get up on Piper, even though blood was dripping from his shoulder onto his saddle. Bud was feeling funny. He couldn't tell if it was from the gunshot or the whiskey, but something about him wasn't right. He had never felt this way before and it scared him.

"Come on, Piper, faster," Bud clucked. Piper started running. They passed the waterworks building where several people were by the river. Bud heard someone say, "Look at that. What in the world is it?"

Bud didn't know what they were talking about. His mind was too fuzzy to think.

Through dazed eyes Bud saw someone standing in the road. It was Elmer Jenkins looking at Bud like he was looking at a ghost. When

Bud and Piper reached him, Elmer jumped in the bushes next to the road, covering his head.

Bud didn't stop, urging Piper on. Blood flowed down his chest and back and his vision was almost gone. His grasp on the reins was loosening.

Ahead of him was a lantern burning on the front porch of Mrs. Harvey's house. In a daze he saw Mrs. Harvey run into her house and slam the door. Yelling something about a crazed spirit.

Piper was blowing and blowing, getting tired, but Bud kicked him and the horse responded.

Bud and Piper were getting closer to home. Their farm was half a mile ahead of them when they passed Mr. William Black's house.

Bud thought to stop at Mr. Black's and send him to fetch his family, but as he neared the house, he saw Mr. Black running yelling, "Don't stop here devil, don't stop here!"

Bud couldn't think straight. Where was he? Where was he going? Why were those people all acting so strange? He kept hearing a clicking noise. What could it be? He wondered if he was dreaming. It felt like floating into the sky.

The next morning Bud's family found Piper grazing in the back yard. Bud was dead, slumped over the horn of his saddle. Blood was everywhere.

The McCrystal men decided to retrace Bud's trip home. They stopped first at Mr. Black's, he was working in his garden.

"Mr. Black, did you see my son Charles last night?" Papa McCrystal asked.

"I saw him yesterday afternoon around three o'clock but I didn't see him last night. I'll tell you what I did see last night, though you probably won't believe me."

"What was that?"

"I saw a horse running by that had sparks flying out from between its legs. The devil was riding him. Scared me so bad I ran in the house. I'm sure it was the devil."

"Could it have been Charles riding Piper?"

"No, it was a demon riding an evil horse. It couldn't have been Charles."

"We found Charles dead on his horse this morning in our back yard. He had been shot."

"Oh, no, that's terrible news. My condolences to you. Charles was a good boy."

"Yes, he was Mr. Black. Thank you for saying so."

The McCrystal men walked on down Mackville Road until they came to Mrs. Harvey's where she was sitting on the front porch.

"What did I do to deserve a visit from all you good-looking McCrystal men?"

"Mrs. Harvey, did you see Charles pass last night?"

"No, I saw him yesterday afternoon, but I didn't see him last night. He promised he would stop on his way home from town and pay me for some moonshine he drank. But he didn't! That Bud, he's a charmer."

She continued, "You know what I did see last night? You won't believe me if I tell you."

"What did you see Mrs. Harvey?"

"I saw a horse running down the road that had sparks flying out between its legs. A red devil was riding it. I ran into the house because I was afraid of seeing it again. You don't believe me, do you?"

"We don't doubt your story, Mrs. Harvey, although we're sad to tell you that Charles is dead."

"Oh no! How did he die?"

"He was shot. He bled to death before he reached the house."

"Oh no, my sweet blue-eyed boy taken down in his prime. I'll miss him so," Mrs. Harvey said as she started to cry.

The men took leave of Mrs. Harvey and headed on to town.

"How can it be that both Mrs. Harvey and Mr. Black experienced the same supernatural occurrence?"

"It seems impossible. I don't understand it."

"Neither do I."

"Well, it was a full moon last night and sometimes that full moon makes things look different."

Shortly they arrived at Mr. Elmer Jenkins' farm. He was in his front field sawing up logs.

"Good morning, Elmer, could we talk to you a minute?"

"Of course you can. What can I do for you?"

"Did you see my son Charles ride by here last night?"

"No, I didn't see Charles anytime yesterday because I wasn't home. I took Mrs. Jenkins to Cornishville to see her sister. We left early and got back late. Why are you asking?"

"Charles was shot and killed last night. We found him dead on his horse in the backyard this morning."

Elmer shook his head and said, "I hate to hear that. I thought a lot of Bud."

"We know you did. He thought a lot of you too."

"Oh, before you go, can I tell you all about something?"

"What is it, Elmer?"

"Last night I saw a horse running past the farm that had sparks flying out between its leg's. A red devil was riding him. I jumped in the bushes and hid until it passed. I know it sounds crazy but I was as sober as you are now. I ran to the house and my wife asked me what was wrong with me. She said,

"You look like you've seen a ghost."

"I didn't tell her what I had seen. I didn't want to scare her."

"You did right by not telling her, Elmer. No use in worrying the womenfolk."

"So, do you all believe my story?"

"We wouldn't doubt anything you said Elmer."

"When is the funeral going to be?" He asked the McCrystals.

"Tomorrow afternoon. We put Charles body in the root cellar to keep it cool. Trying to bury him today would have been too much."

"I understand, I'll see you all tomorrow."

The McCrystals continued the walk toward town. As they were crossing the bridge over Salt River they heard talking. Looking over the railing they saw two vagabonds camping.

"Hello, down there."

The vagabonds looked up at the men.

Papa McCrystal asked them, "Did you see a man ride by here on a horse last night? The man had been shot and probably wasn't riding balanced on his horse."

One of the vagabonds answered, "We saw the devil riding a horse across the bridge that had sparks flying out between its legs. The sparks lit the road up. It was spooky. Have you ever seen anything like that?"

The McCrystals assured the men they hadn't.

"Thank you for talking to us. We appreciate it," they said as they walked away.

The vagabonds waved.

The men stood in the shade of a sycamore tree.

"What are we going to tell the women folk when we get home?"

"We'll tell them no one saw Charles riding home last night, because no one did."

"What about the sparks flying under the horse's legs, being ridden by the devil?"

"We won't be telling them that story either. They don't need to know it."

"What do you think the sparks between the horse's legs were?"

"It must have been a forewarning of death to come."

"Did the sparks come from then devil?"

"No, not the devil, but it was something beyond this world."

They buried Charles the next day and John Macinaw was arrested for murder.

It was later assumed that Pipers shoes had come loose, perhaps when he was kicking out from the strike of Macinaw's whip. With the metal horseshoes striking each other as the horse galloped down the road and the brightness of the moon reflecting on them, the shoes set off sparks that the people had seen.

Bud, covered with blood, appeared to look red to those who saw him.

Old Man Peters

1921

Old Man Peters lived alone way down in the country. He was aloof and mean to everybody who passed his way. People said he was as sour as green apple cider.

Occasionally, he would talk to Preacher Smith. He once told the preacher he planned to never leave his farm. Not even after he died.

One day the neighbors noticed they hadn't seen Old Man Peters outside for over a week.

"Should we go check on him?"

"He's libel to shoot us."

"It's not like him to let his garden go. I think we should check on him."

"You go in first, in case he shoots at us."

"Hello, hello, Mr. Peters are you in there?"

They listened for an answer or the sound of a shotgun being loaded. They opened the front door and saw Old Man Peter's dead body on the kitchen floor. He was holding a razor in his hand, a dirty towel in the other hand and half of his face was covered with dried up soap.

They buried him at Upper Creek Baptist Church Cemetery. Preacher Smith preached a good sermon for Mr. Peters. It wasn't easy to think of nice things to say about him, but somehow Preacher Smith managed to.

A few months later the county sold his farm to the highest bidder at an auction. Mr. and Mrs. Garnett Ashley bought it for two hundred and fifteen dollars. Recently married, they were excited about their new farm.

They moved into the house on a Thursday and by nighttime they had most of their possessions set into place.

Around midnight they both heard a loud thump in the kitchen. Mr. Garnett went to investigate the situation. The front door was locked and there wasn't anyone in the house. He figured it was a raccoon that jumped off a tree onto the roof of the house. That's what he told his wife and they went back to sleep.

The next morning as Mrs. Ashley fixed breakfast, she noticed her husband shaving over the dry sink. It dawned on her he was wearing a red checkered shirt.

"Where did you get that shirt at?" she asked him.

When she turned for the answer, there wasn't anyone there.

She walked over to the window and looked outside for her husband. She saw him in the barn lot.

"Garnett were you just in here shaving?"

"No, I shaved yesterday. I didn't need to shave today. Why?"

"I saw you or someone standing at the dry sink shaving."

"When?"

"Just now! When I looked back you or someone was gone."

"Well, it wasn't me, I've been in the barn for thirty minutes."

"Who was it then if it wasn't you?"

"You must have imagined it."

"I didn't imagine it. I saw a man wearing a red checkered shirt. He was shaving his face."

"There isn't anyone here now, I think it will be all right. Finish fixing breakfast. I'll be right in."

"All right."

That afternoon Mrs. Ashley cleaned the glass of a little mirror the previous owner had left. She rubbed the mirrors surface and soon it shined like brand new. She admired her work and looked at her image, then hung the mirror back on the wall.

From the corner of her eye, she caught sight of a reflection in the mirror. It wasn't her reflection. Staring back at her was an angry old man.

Mrs. Ashley screamed and ran out of the house. Her husband ran in from the corn field.

"What's the matter?"

"I saw the reflection of an old man in the mirror. I think it was the same man I saw shaving!"

"What are you talking about woman?"

"That mirror in the house is haunted. This house is haunted!"

"No, it's not. You aren't used to this place yet. I assure you this house is not haunted."

They went back into the house and all was calm. The mirror hung straight in its place. When they checked the reflection all they saw was themselves.

Around midnight they heard the loud thump in the kitchen again.

"What is that?" She asked her husband with fear in her voice.

"It must be a coon jumping down from a tree. I was so busy with everything else today I forgot to look for coon tracks on the roof. I'll look tomorrow."

The next morning Mrs. Ashley was sweeping up the kitchen floor when she heard water being poured. When she turned to look, an old man was standing there shaving.

"What in God's name do you want?" She screamed at him.

The old man ignored her and continued shaving. She reached for her rolling pin and threw it as hard as she could across the room directly at him. It passed straight through his body, and hit the far wall of the house. The old man's body disappeared down into the floorboards.

Mrs. Ashley walked over to the spot on the floor and touched it with her hand. The wood floor was cold as ice.

Mr. Ashley came in the house.

"Garnett, we have to move from here."

"Why?"

"I just saw the old man's ghost again. I am not living in a house with a ghost."

"But we just bought the place."

"I won't spend another night here. You can take me to my Mother's house until you sell this haunted house."

"It might not be easy to sell it for a profit."

"Sell it at a loss, I won't be back here."

"Are you sure about this?"

"I won't be back here Garnett."

It took nearly a month to sell the farm. Mr. Ashley contacted the backup bidder from the auction and they agreed on a price. Two hundred dollars even, a fifth-teen dollar loss.

"Why did you buy this place then turn around and sell it?" The buyer asked Garnett.

"My wife didn't like it here. Too far from town. She missed seeing her Mother. So, to keep her happy, we will live closer to town."

"When can we move in?"

"You can move in today."

The new family, Mr. and Mrs. Tom Brownfield were eager to move in. Mr. Ashley wished them well and rode away on his horse.

Mr. and Mrs. Brownfield were pleased with the house. The Ashley's had left it clean and tidy. The morning was uneventful as they placed their furniture where they wanted it.

Mrs. Brownfield hung curtains in the windows and swept the floor. She noticed a small mirror the Ashley's had left on the kitchen wall so she walked over to it.

She looked directly into the mirror and saw the face of an old man staring back at her. She screamed and ran out the door. Mr. Brownfield ran to the house.

"What happened?" He called out.

His wife was crying.

"What is the matter with you?"

"I saw a ghost in the house."

"What did you say woman?"

"I said I saw a ghost in the house."

135

"You must have been dreaming."

"No, I wasn't. I looked into the mirror and an old man's face looked back at me."

"I want to see this for myself."

"Go ahead, I'll wait out here."

Mr. Brownfield went into the house and walked over to the mirror. He expected to see nothing but his own reflection. When he looked into the mirror an old man was staring back at him.

"Who in God's name are you?"

The old man's face disappeared from the mirrors image.

Mr. Brownfield went out to the yard where his wife was crying.

"Well, what did you see?" she asked him.

"I don't believe it, but I saw an old man's face staring back at me."

"Oh no!" Mrs. Brownfield cried out.

"Calm down, calm down, the mirror must have a curse on it. I'll take it down and break it into little pieces."

"No, you can't do that. Breaking a mirror brings seven years bad luck. Breaking a cursed mirror could bring endless bad luck."

"What do you want me to do?"

"Let's go talk to the Henry's. They are Catholic, maybe they will understand how to deal with such a thing."

The Brownfield's walked down Oakland Lane to the Henry farm. Albert Henry and Richard Henry were working in a corn field when they arrived.

"Excuse me Mr. Henry, could I talk to you a minute?"

Albert walked over to the fence. "What can I do for you sir?"

"My name is Samuel Brownfield, this is my wife, Elizabeth."

"Nice to meet you," Albert said.

Mr. Brownfield continued. "We bought the Ashley's farm, Old Man Peter's place."

"I wondered who had bought the farm. So, it's you and your pretty wife."

"Yes, sir, that's right," Samuel said.

"Well, what did you need to know Samuel?"

"Have you ever heard of Old Man Peters house being haunted?"

"Have you folks been seeing a ghost over there?"

"Yes, we have, I hate to admit."

"How did the ghost appear to you?" Albert asked the Brownfield's.

"We both saw an old man's face in a mirror."

"What did he look like?" Richard asked.

"He was an old man with a rough complexion He had a bald head and a wart on the side of his nose. He was wearing a red checkered jacket."

"Sounds like Old Man Peters to me," Albert said.

Mrs. Brownfield started to cry again. She sat down on the ground and fainted. The men tapped her on the face, and after a minute she came to.

"I'm sure Father Caldwell can help with your problem," Albert told them.

"Really? Do you think so?" Mrs. Brownfield asked the Henry men.

"I'm sure he can. I'll go fetch him for you right now," Richard told her.

"Why don't you young folks go wait up at my house until he comes back."

"That would be too much trouble Mr. Henry."

"It's no trouble at all. Your wife needs to cool off and drink some water."

"Thank you, we will go up to your house."

The Brownfield's walked up to the Henry's house. Elizabeth sat down in a chair on the porch while Samuel got her a drink of water from the well.

Albert and Richard's Mother, Mrs. Henry looked out the door. "May I help you with something?"

"Hello, I am Samuel Brownfield, this is my wife, Elizabeth. We talked to your son Albert out in the corn field. He asked us to wait here on the porch for him."

"And what does this matter concern?"

"You see Mrs. Henry, we saw a ghost at our house, and we are afraid to go back home."

"I see, I see."

"Your son Richard has gone to get the priest for us. He said the priest would help us."

"I'm sure he can, Father Caldwell is very close to God."

Shortly, Albert, Richard and Father Caldwell came walking up the lane.

Richard has told me your story. We will go bless your house," Father Caldwell told the Brownfield's.

"Oh, thank you so much," Elizabeth said.

They all walked to the Brownfield's farm. Elizabeth made it very clear that she would wait outside until the ghost was gone. Samuel, Albert, Richard and Father Caldwell went into the house.

Father Caldwell put his blessed robe on over his clothes. He lit a sacred candle and began to pray. He blessed the whole house with holy water.

"Where is the mirror that holds the ghost?"

Samuel pointed to it on the wall.

When Father Caldwell looked into the mirror, he took a step backwards.

"What in God's name do you want?" He made the sign of the cross.

"What is it Father Caldwell?" Albert asked.

"I saw an old man's face in the mirror. It was Mr. Peters. It has disappeared now."

"Oh, my word!" Samuel exclaimed, "Is there any hope of ridding the house of his spirit?"

"Yes," Father Caldwell assured him.

"Have you seen the ghost anywhere else besides in the mirror?" Albert asked.

"No, I haven't, but my wife has. She saw his ghost in the kitchen twice. He appeared to be shaving."

"I know what's going on here Father," Albert said.

"What is it, Albert?"

"Old Man Peters was found dead on the floor with a razor in his hand. There was dried soap on one side his face, so he had been shaving. He had been looking into that mirror when he died."

"What are you saying?" Samuel asked Albert.

"What I'm saying is this. Everyone knows to cover the mirrors in the house with black material when someone dies. If you don't, the spirit will see its reflection and become trapped in the mirror, unable to go on to heaven."

"What do you think Father?"

"Though the church would never approve of it, I have heard about that superstition all my life."

"What shall we do?" Samuel pleaded.

"I say we break the mirror into little pieces. That way Mr. Peters spirit can escape from it. What do you think Father?" Albert asked.

"I believe if I bless the mirror, then break it into tiny pieces, Mr. Peters soul and spirit could go on to heaven and stop haunting this house."

"When can we start?" Samuel asked.

"Right away," Father answered.

Father Caldwell took the mirror off the wall and laid it flat on the kitchen table.

He used his holy water and blessed the mirror three times.

"Father, who is going to break the mirror? I don't want seven years bad luck," Richard said.

"After being blessed, the mirror will not emit any bad luck."

"Let's take it outside and break it up."

Elizabeth was still sitting on the front porch.

"What are you doing with the mirror?"

"We are going to break it into tiny pieces," Albert told her.

"Then you will have seven years of bad luck!"

"No Elizabeth, Father Caldwell assured us that a blessed article wouldn't bring bad luck. He believes Mr. Peter's spirit and soul are trapped in this mirror, and by breaking it up, he will be free to leave this world."

"How did his spirit become trapped in the mirror?" Elizabeth asked.

"He was shaving his face, looking into the mirror, when he died. Mr. Peters saw his reflection in the mirror as he passed away. That caused his spirit to become trapped in the mirror. You always cover a mirror when someone dies."

"My family cover the mirrors in our homes when someone passes away," Elizabeth said, "I believe in it."

They took the mirror to barn and put it inside of an empty feed sack. Albert, Richard and Samuel hit the feed sack with hammers. Samuel picked up a sledgehammer and hit the sack with all his might.

"That will do," Father Caldwell told them.

"Now what Father?"

"Pour the glass out on this burlap bag."

Samuel poured it out. The glass was ground to the point of being the size of grains of sand.

"Stand back now so his spirit can leave."

The men stepped back away from the broken glass lying on the burlap bag. At the same time, they saw a white mist rise up from the broken glass and disappear into thin air.

"Elizabeth, the crisis has passed, the ghost is gone," Samuel told his wife.

"Oh, thank you Father. We will be forever in your debt."

After that day there weren't any more sightings of Mr. Peters.

Tap Tap

1924

After Grandpa Leonard died, Grandma Leonard moved to town. Her three unmarried daughters, Minnie, Pearlie and Vivian moved with her. She purchased a nice house on Mooreland Ave, one of the main streets leading into Harrodsburg. It was a good location for entertaining, and they loved to entertain.

They enjoyed playing the piano, singing, reciting poetry during afternoon teas or just visiting on the front porch. Grandma Leonard and her daughters hosted the local Women's Garden club, and the Sunday School meetings on Thursday nights. If they had company, the women were happy. Visitors were always welcome.

During that era, people enjoyed experiencing supernatural occurrences. Many were afraid of contacting dead spirits, but the Leonard women held séances to try to communicate with the dead.

They played with Ouija Boards, read Tarot cards, and even attempted levitation's on willing participants. They considered these activities to be parlor games. One of their favorite games was talking to the dead.

Grandma Leonard didn't participate in these activities, but she didn't see any harm in her girls doing it. She still had hopes of getting her three girls married, and she figured the more callers they had, the better chance the girls had of finally getting a husband. So she allowed the girls to participate in just about anything, as long as it was proper.

One Saturday afternoon their Aunt Maggie stopped by to visit them. Aunt Maggie was Grandma Leonards sister. Her husband, William Brown had died three months earlier and Aunt Maggie was still in mourning.

Aunt Maggie had endured a terrible life. Soon after they were married, William Brown began to show a different side to himself. He said hateful, hurtful things to Aunt Maggie and the children, Rebecca and William Jr, just to make them feel bad. He slapped them around when he felt like it and never showed them any respect. William Brown badgered his family endlessly.

He was a lawyer by occupation and with his ability to argue anyone under the table, he seldom lost a case. He was known to be mean, unscrupulous, cold hearted and smart. People respected him out of fear.

William Brown knew how to sway the jury over to his side. He knew the questions to ask witnesses that would put them on the spot.

Once, when a well-known liar took the stand against one of Williams clients, William asked him, "Do you consider yourself a honest upright citizen?"

Everyone in the jury and the courtroom started laughing. They already knew the witnesses character, but William had pointed it out to them anyway. William's client was found innocent.

Another time he asked a man who was a witness against his client, "Have you ever been accused of being a chicken thief?"

Knowing well the man had spent two years in prison for stealing chickens. The witness answered he didn't know anything about chickens or the defendant. And wasn't sure why he had been called to court in the first place because he didn't know nothing about the case.

William asked for dismissal of the charge against his client and the judge agreed. The prosecutors shook their heads in disbelief. William shook his clients hand.

His children, Rebecca and William Jr. were very intelligent. Verging on the edge of being geniuses. Excelling at school in every subject and category. They were musically inclined, being able to play six different instruments. They played the Piano and the Pump Organ, and an Accordion. They strummed Guitars, Mandolins and Banjos. They provided the music at most of the towns social events and at their church on Sundays and Wednesday nights.

Any money they received from a social event for the musical entertainment, went directly to their father.

One time William Jr., entered a Burma Shave poetry contest. He wrote the slogan, "Our cream is like a parachute, there isn't any substitute." He won the contest and a check for one thousand dollars, a tremendous amount of money for the time. William Jr. dreamed of how he would spend his money. But when the check arrived, William Sr. took all of the money and William Jr. never saw one dollar of it.

William Brown continued to push his family too hard. It was said he beat them with a singletree broken off of a harness.

In their teenage years, both children were admitted to a Sanitarium for emotional disorders caused by the years of mental and physical abuse.

Several months after they were admitted, Rebecca committed suicide by drinking lye. They said she had to be in terrible agony, but instead, she died laughing.

After her death, William Jr. refused to eat and eventually starved himself to death lying on a bed with his left arm handcuffed to the headboard.

Aunt Maggie was relieved her children had passed on. The life they had in the Sanitarium was worse than no life at all. She had begged her husband to move the children to a better facility, but he refused. He told her it didn't matter where they were because they were crazy anyway.

When the news reached town of Rebecca's death and then William Jr's death, Aunt Maggie felt ashamed. She felt it was her fault her daughter and son were dead. The folks around town knew who she lived with and no one blamed her for anything.

Two years later, William Brown dropped dead from a heart attack while arguing a case in front of a jury. They say he grabbed his chest and cursed the Lord as he fell, hitting his head on the witnesses chair.

A large crowd attended his funeral, more out of respect for Aunt Maggie then for him. They buried him at Bruners Chapel Cemetery, being he willed Bruners Chapel the majority of his money and left Aunt Maggie a small monthly trust. An insult, considering the amount of money he had. Even in his death he treated her badly.

Several months had passed since his funeral and Aunt Maggie had moved to town from the country. She didn't feel safe being alone so far from town. She made arrangements to rent a nice room at Mrs. Deans Boarding house, in exchange for cleaning the house on a daily basis.

Though she missed her children terribly, she was as content as she had been since she was a child. No more fear. No more abuse.

* * * *

Now, back to that Saturday afternoon at Grandma Leonards house. Around four o'clock the girls joined their Mother and their Aunt inside. The afternoon sun was hitting the front porch, so it was time to go in for a while.

Vivian, Minnie and Pearlie decided to take a nap. Grandma Leonard and Aunt Maggie talked in the kitchen while they fixed supper.

After supper it began to rain, ruining the girls plans. They had planned to sit on the front porch to see and talk to people who were out and about on a Saturday night. But no one would be out walking in a downpour for them to see or talk to, so they convinced Aunt Maggie to spend the night with them, instead of walking home in the rain. She agreed to stay.

A new set of stereo-optic cards featuring National Parks of America had arrived in the mail that day and they all enjoyed looking at them. It was still early in the evening when Vivian suggested.

"Let's ask the table questions."

"What do you mean?" Aunt Maggie asked.

"Oh, the girls try to communicate with the dead, using the little walnut table for the medium. You know the table, the one our Grandpa made from the walnut tree on his farm that was struck by lightning." Grandma Leonard told her sister.

"That sounds scary to me," Aunt Maggie replied.

"It's not scary, it's fun," Vivian told her Aunt.

"Get the table Minnie," Vivian told her sister.

Minnie brought the table to the center of the parlor and sat it on the middle of the rug.

"What do we do now?" Aunt Maggie asked.

"We ask the table to be our medium. Then we ask it questions. The table only taps if the answer is yes. If the answer is no, there isn't any reply. It's better to speak to someone who has recently passed away, because their spiritual powers seem stronger," Vivian said.

"Who should we call up first?" Minnie asked.

"Mrs. Tewmey died last week. Let's try to contact her," Vivian replied, then said,

"Now everyone concentrate on Mrs. Tewmey. Think hard, remember how she looked, how she talked. Then I'll ask the questions. Mrs. Tewmey, are you here with us tonight?"

To Aunt Maggie's surprise the table began to teeter back and forth.

Vivian continued. "Mrs. Tewmey are you in heaven?"

The table tapped its leg against the floor.

"I'm not sure I want to see anymore," Aunt Maggie told her nieces.

"Its alright, don't be scared Aunt Maggie," Pearlie told her Aunt.

Vivian asked the next question,"Mrs. Tewmey, is Mr. Tewmey in heaven with you?"

The table didn't move.

"Mr. Tewmey must not have made it to heaven," Vivian commented.

"He was a mean old cuse," Grandma Leonard added. And the others agreed with her.

"Let's talk to someone else," Minnie suggested.

"First, let me thank Mrs. Tewmey for communicating with us. Thank you, Mrs. Tewmey. We are glad that you are in heaven."

"Who else has died lately Mother?" Vivian asked.

"Mr. Carl Simpson passed over a few weeks ago. I wouldn't expect him to be in heaven. He never stepped a foot into a church in his life," Grandma Leonard replied.

"Try to contact him Vivian," Pearlie said.

"Alright, think about Mr. Simpson, remember what he looked like." Vivian began to talk to the table.

"Mr. Simpson are you here with us tonight?" The table tapped its leg.

"He's here," Aunt Maggie said in a scared voice.

"Mr. Simpson, are you in heaven?" The table tapped its leg again.

"Mr. Simpson is in heaven!" Minnie exclaimed.

"Mother, I thought you said he wouldn't go to heaven if he didn't go to church?" Grandma Leonard knew she had to think of an answer fast. Being she had instilled in her children that without church on earth there wouldn't be eternity in heaven.

"Maybe Mr. Simpson prayed alone. He may have not felt comfortable being in a church. I guarantee if he is in heaven, he knew God during his life."

"Ask him if he had God in his life."

"Mr. Simpson? Did you have God in your life?"

The table tapped against the floor.

"I guess you are right mother." The girls replied in unison.

"Mr. Simpson? Is heaven as pretty as the bible says it is?" The table answered yes.

"Thank you Mr. Simpson. We are glad that you are in heaven."

"Who else can we call up?" Pearlie asked.

"I know someone," Minnie said.

"Who is it?" Vivian asked.

"Cousin Rebecca."

"Oh no, don't do that," Aunt Maggie cried out. "I can't bear to hear from her."

"It might make you feel better," Grandma Leonard commented.

"How could it make me feel better?"

"It might bring you peace of mind."

"I don't know."

"It will be o.k. Aunt Maggie. Actually we've talked to her before. Mother told us not to tell you about it."

"What did she say about being in heaven?" Aunt Maggie asked her niece.

"The table said she was in heaven."

"Oh my Lord," Aunt Maggie started crying. "I was afraid she went to hell. Being she took her own life."

Grandma Leonard patted her sisters back and said, "God wouldn't punish Rebecca, she didn't know what she was doing. In fact, I believe the poor souls who were lost on earth, are found in heaven."

"Let's talk to her," Aunt Maggie said.

Vivian began. "Cousin Rebecca are you with us tonight?"

The table tapped against the floor.

"She's here Aunt Maggie, she's here," Vivian exclaimed.

"Ask her if she is alright."

"Are you alright Cousin Rebecca?"

The table replied that she was.

"Ask if her brother is with her?"

"Cousin Rebecca is Cousin William with you?" The table answered yes.

"Oh I am so relieved," Aunt Maggie said. There was a tear in her eye, not from being sad, but from being happy.

"Vivian, ask her if her mind is straight, now that she is in heaven."

"Cousin Rebecca is your mind clear now?" The table tapped yes.

"Cousin Rebecca, do you love your mother?" Again the table replied yes.

"Are you happy in heaven?" The answer was yes.

"I'm so glad they are in heaven together. Tell them I love them and will see them when I get to heaven," Aunt Maggie proclaimed.

"Do you want to talk to William?" Vivian asked.

"Of course I do. I love him too."

"William are you happy in heaven?" Tap tap, the table replied.

Aunt Maggie was so relieved. Part of her pain had weakened knowing her children were in heaven with the Lord.

Grandma Leonard told her girls, "That's enough for tonight. Put the table back where it belongs." Then she and Aunt Maggie went into the kitchen.

Minnie picked the table up.

"Don't put it back yet," Vivian said.

"But Mother told us too," Minnie replied.

"I know she did. But I'm not ready to quit quiet yet."

"Who else are you thinking about communicating with?" Pearlie asked her sister.

"I have someone in mind," Vivian answered.

"Well who is it Vivian?"

"William Brown, Aunt Maggie's husband?"

"Why would you want to talk to him? He's not in heaven Vivian." Minnie said.

"If he could get to heaven, anyone could," Pearlie commented.

"I don't think Mother or Aunt Maggie would want us to," Minnie told her sisters.

"They are in the kitchen. They'll never know it," Vivian insisted.

"Come on, let's call for him."

"O.K. sister. Go ahead."

"He's not going to answer because he's not in heaven," Minnie insisted to Vivian and Pearlie.

"Come on now, remember what he looked like. Think about the sound of his voice."

"Uncle William, Uncle William, are you there?"

The girls waited for an answer but nothing happened.

"See, I told you he wasn't in heaven," Pearlie said.

"Just be patient, I'll ask again. Uncle William, Uncle William, are you there?"

They looked at the table and at first they didn't realize what was going on. Pearlie reached for Minnie's hand, Minnie reached for Vivian's hand and Vivian reached for Pearlie's hand.

The table was vibrating violently on the floor, emitting a humming sound. All of a sudden, the table flew across the room, hitting the piano, breaking it to pieces. The girls screamed.

Grandma Leonard and Aunt Maggie came running into the parlor.

"What's going on in here?" Grandma asked. "How did the table get broken? Did you throw it across the room?"

The sisters didn't answer.

Vivian took a deep breath and Minnie and Pearlie started crying.

"You had better have a good reason for breaking the table. Were you standing on it?"

"No mother, we were not standing on it."

"How did it get broken then?"

"The table flew across the room on it's own," Vivian said.

"What do you mean Vivian?"

"I'm telling you Mother, the table started vibrating. Making a noise that sounded like a swarm of bee's. Didn't it Sisters?" Minnie and Pearlie agreed.

"This is very hard for me to believe daughters. None of it makes any sense. If you broke the table by accident, admit it to me now and your punishment won't be as harsh."

"Mother, we didn't break the table. It flew across the room, just like I said it did," Vivian replied.

"Tell me this," Grandma said. "Were you communicating with someone when this incident occurred?"

"Yes, we were."

"Who were you talking too? Vivian, answer my question."

"We were trying to talk to Uncle William."

Aunt Maggie gasped for air and fell back into a chair. Her skin was white as snow.

"Get your Aunt a glass of water."

Minnie went to get the water while Grandma Leonard patted Aunt Maggie's hand. Vivian fanned her face with the newspaper and Pearlie rubbed her legs.

"Calm down now, everything is alright."

Aunt Maggie sipped the water and soon the color started returning to her face.

Grandma Leonard asked her daughters, "Why would you girls want to talk to your Uncle? After knowing how he treated your Aunt and Cousins?"

"We just happened to think of him," Vivian replied.

"We didn't mean to do any harm Mother. It was only a game," Minnie added.

"Your game went very wrong. You asked to talk to the wrong person. If anyone is in hell with the devil, it's your Uncle William. The devil came through the table when you called out his name. Only an evil spirit would cause so much destruction."

Everyone agreed with Grandma Leonard.

"Minnie, you and Pearlie pick up the table. Vivian, you help me carry the table to the burn pile."

"It's raining outside Mother."

"I know it is. Maybe some of Gods blessed rain will wash away the evil."

Aunt Maggie sat in the chair sipping her water and fanning her face. Minnie and Pearlie swept up pieces of the broken table that had scattered across the floor. Grandma Leonard and Vivian carried the pieces of the broken table to the burn pile. Grandma poured gasoline on the burn pile and sat it on fire.

After that incident, Vivian tried to communicate with the dead through other tables, but she wasn't ever able to do it again.

Swept Clean

1925

Mom and Papa Henry moved their family from farm to farm. Always looking for a better house and more tillable land.

They heard of a farm on Oakland Lane that was for rent. It had a fairly nice house and a good-sized barn. There were rumors of the house being haunted, but the rent was reasonable. Mom and Papa figured if they hung a crucifix in the house that would rid it of evil spirits.

They moved in on a Thursday. Bringing their possessions on a wagon, along with their chickens. Everyone worked hard to get settled in.

Being there were ten people in the family the rooms were divided up for bedrooms. Three of the girls, Rosa, Lillie and Isabel would share a room. Rhetha, Mattie and Susie got the second bedroom. Mom and Papa got the third bedroom and John and Cecil turned the attic into their bedroom.

Isabel put her holy cards on the wall of her bedroom for decoration. Rosa and Lillie thought the holy cards added color to the room and were pleased.

That night after supper, Rosa and Isabel explored the barn where they found a baby chicken with a deformed leg.

"The poor little thing, he can barely walk. Let's take him to house. Mom can probably fix his leg," Rosa said.

They carried the little chicken into the kitchen.

"Mom, Mom, we found a little hurt chicken. Can You help it?" Isabel asked.

"Don't bring that bird into the house. Don't you know that a bird in the house is a bad omen? What is wrong with you? Take the chicken back to the barn."

"We're sorry Mom. We didn't know it was bad. Can we try to fix its leg?"

"Yes, but not in the house."

Rosa and Isabel took the baby chick back to the barn. They took a small stick and tied it on the chick's leg with a piece of string like a splint. The chick didn't seem to mind at all. They named the chick, 'White Feather.'

There was a wooden box in the barn that they made into a nest for White Feather. Filling it with soft pieces of cloth they placed the little chick in it. He settled down right away.

That night after everyone had gone to bed a terrible thunderstorm erupted. Strong winds blew the rain sideways and rattled the windows.

"I'm worried about White Feather. He could drown in his nest. Let's go get him," Rosa told her two sisters.

"I don't think we should. Mom said it was a bad omen to have a bird in the house," Lillie said.

"What could it hurt? I agree with Rosa. White Feather could drown in the barn tonight. I vote to go get him," Isabel said.

"I'll go get him. I'll climb out the window. Isabel, you and Lillie keep an eye out for Mom and Papa."

Rosa put a jacket over her head and climbed out the window. Before long she returned with White Feather.

"Let's go back to bed. We can put White Feather between us to keep him warm."

"Leave the lamp on. I want to pet White Feather for a few minutes."

There was an ordinary house broom leaning in the corner of the room. Suddenly, the broom flew up into the air and swept its bristles across the girl's heads. It continued to fly around the room. It moved horizontally toward the wall and swept Isabel's holy cards off the wall.

All three of the girls started to scream.

Papa and Cecil ran into the room. They saw the broom hovering close to the ceiling. Papa tried to grab it but the broom hit him in the head. Cecil reached out to grab it but couldn't catch it. The broom moved too fast.

The girls hid underneath the bed covers and cried.

"Do something Papa!"

The broom flew around the room. It swooped down then returned to the ceiling.

Papa stood on a chair to try and reach the broom, but it flew down and knocked him off the chair.

Mom Henry came into the room.

"What in the world is going on in here?"

The broom was swirling around and around. Papa grabbed at it again and this time he caught it. The handle was hot as fire. He dropped it to the floor and stepped on it.

"Girls, give me your blanket."

Lillie tossed him the blanket. He covered the broom with the blanket and carried it out of the room. He struggled to keep it in his hands. The broom tried to escape his grasp. He took it to the fireplace and tossed it in the burning embers. Papa held the broom down with an iron poker and it caught fire immediately. The handle and straw crackled and popped until it became part of the burning embers.

Papa heard Mom yelling in the girl's bedroom. He hurried back in fear another supernatural occurrence was happening.

"If it wasn't raining so hard, I would take all three of you outside and whip you with a switch!"

"What is it?" Papa asked.

"These girls brought that crippled chicken in the house! No wonder there is evil in this room! Cecil, you take that chicken back to the barn right now!"

"It's raining hard Mom."

"Then you will get wet! Get that bird out of my house right now!"

Cecil took White Feather off the bed and carefully carried him out.

"There won't be any more talk tonight. I'll deal with you girls in the morning."

The first thing the next morning the girls went to check on White Feather. They searched everywhere in the barn but couldn't find him.

"Mom, we can't find White Feather. Where do you think he could be?" Rosa asked.

Mom wouldn't answer her.

"Please Mom, help us find him."

Mom turned around and gave the girls a mean look.

"Are you going to give us a whipping Mom?"

"No, I'm not going to give you a whipping. Your punishment is you lost your chicken. When you brought the bird into the house you also brought in evil. The broom was possessed by a witch. I suspect a witch got your chicken. Witches use sickly chickens in their potions. Never, ever bring a bird in the house again. Surely you've learned a lesson."

"We have Mom. We surely have."

Friends Forever

1926

Sally Lay lived with her brother Bill in Dixville, Kentucky. Theirs was a simple life full of hard work. Both in their fifties, neither of them were ever married.

One day while feeding the chickens Sally thought of her best friend from childhood, Anne Taylor. She had a sinking feeling and felt the urge to cry. Sally wondered why she was thinking about Anne, a friend she hadn't seen in thirty-five years.

All that day she thought of Anne. She couldn't get her mind off her. When Bill came in for supper, she mentioned Anne to him.

"It's the funniest thing. I've had Anne Taylor on my mind all day. Wonder why I would be thinking of her?"

"Maybe something just made you think about her."

"No, it's more than that. I have a strange feeling I can't explain."

"When was the last time you saw her?"

"The day she left for Indiana with the traveling salesman. They got married, remember?"

"Yes, I remember."

"We wrote each other fairly often for a while. You know how days turn into weeks and weeks into years and pretty soon you don't write anymore. I haven't had a letter from her in twenty years."

"Well, write her a letter."

"I think I will."

That night Sally dreamed about Anne. She dreamed of the times she and Anne ran through the fields away from Anne's abusive father. She dreamed of how the two girls comforted each other in their times of need. In one of her dreams, she remembered the envy she felt the day Anne married Jim Buster and drove away to Indiana in a wagon full of household goods.

The next morning Sally was breaking beans when someone knocked on the door.

"Who's there?"

"It's your friend forever."

"Who?"

"Anne Taylor. It's Anne Taylor."

"Oh my," Sally said as she jumped up and opened the door.

Sally didn't recognize Anne. She was thin and pale and looked so old.

"Hello Sally. How are you?"

"I don't believe it. I thought about you yesterday. I dreamed about you last night. And here you are on my front porch. Please, Anne, come on in the house. Aren't you cold? Don't you have a coat with you? It is freezing outside."

"I don't need a coat. I don't get cold anymore. I'm starting on my journey."

"Where are you going Anne? Is your husband with you?"

"No, he's in Indiana. He doesn't know I've left."

"What do you mean?"

"I don't mean anything. It's so good to see you Sally. There are several things I want to tell you. Do you remember how we thought Jim Buster was so rich? How he had the wagon full of goods he sold."

"Of course, I remember how rich he was. To tell you the truth, I was jealous of your new life. I always thought about the fine life you were living in Indiana."

"Well, I wasn't living a fine life. In fact, it couldn't have been any worse. When Jim told Daddy he wanted to marry me and Daddy said yes, I thought it was a dream come true. I would be able leave home and not be abused by Daddy anymore. When we got to Indiana, I found out Jim didn't even own the merchandise he sold. He sold it for another man who paid him pennies on the dollar. We lived in a terrible apartment in the city where we froze to death in the winter and burned up in the summer. Many times, we went hungry. Jim was too lazy to try and earn any real money for us. If he ever got any extra money, he spent it on whiskey."

"Oh Anne, I'm sorry to hear that. Do you have any children?"

"No, I never could get pregnant. Jim cursed me for years. He said I wasn't a real woman."

"So, you are leaving him now?"

"I've already left him. He just doesn't know it yet. Sally, I want you to do something for me."

"What is it, Anne?"

"I want you to write to Jim and tell him if he had tried harder to eke out a living, I wouldn't be taking this journey now. I want you to tell him I want my cousin Wilbur to have my pearl necklace that is in my jewelry box."

"Anne, why didn't you tell Jim these things before you left Indiana?"

"I couldn't tell him Sally. I need you to tell him for me."

"Anne, are you expecting to die soon?"

"No one knows when they will die, Sally. It sneaks up on you because you don't see it coming. Dying is easy compared to living in this world."

"You sound bitter Anne."

I'm not bitter, just worn out, that's all."

"Do you want a cup of coffee. We can sit and talk for a while."

"No, I'm not thirsty. I really don't feel anything Sally. I'm not thirsty or hungry or cold. I don't even feel sad. I need to get going. I want to see my cousin Wilbur before I leave. There is one more thing I want you to tell Jim. I hid twenty dollars under the pie safe. It took me fifteen years to save it. I'm sure he can find something to spend it on."

"Where are you going Anne?"

"I don't know where I'm going. I just have a feeling I have to go somewhere."

I hate that you are leaving so soon. I wished we could have visited more. I will write the letter and send it to your husband."

"Thank you, Sally. I need to be on my way. I don't have much time left."

"Maybe you can stop by again sometime soon."

"Maybe I will Sally."

Sally walked out on the porch with Anne. As the two women hugged Sally felt like she was hugging herself. Anne's body was so thin and cold.

"Best friends forever," Sally called out.

"Best friends forever," Anne replied.

Later that afternoon Sally's brother Bill came into the house for supper.

"Guess who came to see me today?"

"Who?"

"Anne Taylor Buster."

"That's strange, being you were thinking about her yesterday."

"It is strange she would show up today."

"How was she?"

"She looked bad, thin and pale. She has left her husband. She told me she was going on a journey but wouldn't tell me where she was going. She said she didn't know where she was going but she was going to stop and see her cousin Wilbur before she left Mercer County."

"That seems peculiar."

"It does. She wants me to write a letter to her husband and tell him he should have worked harder to provide them a better life."

"I don't think it's your place to do that."

"I told her I would."

"We should go talk to her cousin Wilbur. He's her family. If anyone is writing a letter, it should be him."

"Anne said she was going to Wilbur's when she left here."

"Get your coat on and we will walk over to Wilbur's farm."

"All right."

It took thirty minutes to walk to Wilbur's farm. When they arrived, they saw Wilbur up by the barn.

"Wilbur, can we talk to you a minute?"

"Hi, Bill. Hi Sally. What can I do for you?"

"Has Anne gotten here yet?"

"My cousin Anne?"

"Yes."

"I didn't know she was in Dixville. I thought she was in Indiana."

"She stopped by our house this afternoon. She said she was coming over to see you."

"I haven't seen her. If she said she was coming here I'm sure she must be. She probably stopped to visit with someone else first."

"Anne was acting very peculiar. She wants my sister to write a letter to her husband in Indiana. Anne wants Sally to tell him he should have tried harder to make a living for them. She said she wouldn't be making this journey now if he had tried harder. She wants you to have her pearl necklace that's in her jewelry box in Indiana and she wanted me to tell her husband she hid twenty dollars under the pie safe."

"Is Anne dying?"

"We don't know Wilbur."

"I'm sure Anne will explain it all when she gets here."

"Thank you, Wilbur. We will be on our way."

As Bill and Sally turned to leave, they saw Wilbur's son running down the road, yelling.

"Papa, Papa, a telegram has come for you. It must be very important."

Wilbur opened the envelope and began reading the telegram.

FOUND ANNE DEAD THIS MORNING. STOP.
HAD BEEN SICK FOR A WHILE. STOP. WILL
BURY HER IN INDIANA. STOP.

"How can that be? I saw Anne today, I hugged her," Sally cried.

"Somethings don't make sense in life. You must have imagined you saw Anne."

"I saw my friend Anne. Maybe it was her spirit or ghost, but I saw her. I talked to her. Regardless of what you think, Anne came to me today. No one can convince me otherwise."

The Black Dog

1930

Papa Henry and his brother Albert loved to go "Coon" hunting. They each owned coon dogs and were able to recognize each dog's bark. The dogs were let loose to find and tree a raccoon, then the men would follow. Mostly it was a reason to get out in the woods to drink whiskey and tell tall tales without their wives.

One night during a full moon, Papa Henry, Albert and their sons, Cecil, John and William went coon hunting. After they released their dogs, they drank their whiskey and talked around the campfire. It wasn't long until the dogs began to bark, and each man listened intently for his own. Then, from deep in the woods came the sound of a dog that howled above the other dogs.

"What in the world was that? What kind of dog howls like that?" William asked.

"It must be a fox," Cecil said.

"That's not a fox."

"It must be a coyote. What else could it be?"

"It's a wild dog, just let it be."

"Maybe it's the black dog," Albert said quietly.

"What black dog are you talking about?" William asked his Daddy.

"It's the devil's dog. It roams the woods during full moons. It looks for souls to take to hell. If you look directly into its eyes, it will steal your soul when you die."

"I've heard about the black dog," Cecil said. "The first time you see him he will bring you good luck. The second time you see the dog, many sorrows will follow. But that's not the worst, if you see the dog three times, you will die."

"Where did you hear that story at?" William asked his cousin.

"Oh, I've heard that story several times. Papa told me once, remember Papa?"

"Yes, son, I remember."

"Let's go look for the black dog, I could use some good luck," John said.

"I'll go," William called out.

"Me too," Cecil said.

"Come on Papa, let's go look for the black dog."

"I'm not going," Papa said to his son. "I've seen the black dog two times, I don't want to see it again. I don't want to die and go to hell."

"You've already seen the black dog twice? Really? Did you look into its eyes?"

"I've seen the dog twice but I never looked directly into its eyes. I knew better."

"Tell us about it, Papa."

"Well, the first time I saw it I was out hunting with my Papa and my Granddaddy, right here in these woods when we heard the howl of the black dog. They told me the story about the dog. Grandpa and Daddy had seen the black dog twice, and neither of them wanted to see it again because they weren't quite ready to die. But being a young man, I was curious."

"I'm going to look for that black dog," I told Papa and Grandpa.

"Don't scare that dog this way," Grandpa told me.

"It was a full moon that night, just like tonight. I followed a trail down toward the creek and listened for the dog's howl. When I stepped across the creek, a dark shadow fell across me and I fell into the creek. When I started to stand up, the black dog jumped over top of me and landed on the other side of the creek bank. The dog turned and looked at me. I swear boys, when the black dog looked at me with his white eyes, I felt fear in my soul."

"What?" William asked in a surprised voice.

"It's true boy," Uncle Albert said. "Once you've seen those white eyes, you'll never forget them."

"After you saw the dog the first time, did you get any good luck?" Cecil asked his Papa.

"Yes, I did."

"What kind of luck did you get?"

"I remember I got a job cutting hay for real good money."

"What about you Uncle Albert?"

"I had a streak of good luck too."

"What was your luck Uncle Albert?"

"I found a milk cow on Mackville Road. No one ever came to claim her, so I got to keep her. She was an excellent milk producer."

"What about the second time you saw the dog, did you have sorrow Papa?"

"Yes, I did. My Grandmother died two days. She hadn't even been sick. She just fell over and dropped dead."

"What about you Uncle Albert?"

"I experienced the sorrow over Grandma's death too but it wasn't until sometime later I saw the black dog the second time. I was in fear thinking what my sorrow might be."

"What was your sorrow Uncle Albert?"

"A broken heart."

"A broken heart?" The younger men asked in a surprised voice.

"Yes, a broken heart. The girl I had been courting for a year, Elizabeth Curry, died from a black widow spider bite."

"That's sad Uncle Albert."

"Well, let's get going to look for that dog. We could all use some good luck."

John, Cecil and William left the campfire and headed toward the woods. At that exact minute the howl of the black dog filled the air with an eerie sound. The hunting dogs, who had barked all night, suddenly went quiet. The men all stopped dead in their tracks.

"Maybe this isn't a good idea."

"Maybe we should go back to the campfire."

The black dog howled close by.

"Let's go now."

Cecil, John and William ran through the woods toward the campfire. They realized something was chasing them. They ran faster to escape the horror that followed them. Suddenly, their own hunting dogs passed them by headed toward the campfire. William stopped and looked back into the woods.

"Hey fellows, I think we are all right. It was our own dogs chasing us, not the black dog."

Cecil and John slowed down and glanced back at their cousin.

"You're probably right William. We're acting like a bunch of kids, being afraid of some black dog."

The tension in the air subsided and William and Cecil laughed at themselves.

"Come on, let's go back to camp."

John put his arm around William's shoulder and they turned around in unison. Standing directly in front of them, blocking the trail, was the black dog. Its white eyes burned bright as a lantern's white flame. As if it could see in the dark and steal your soul. It howled at them and turned its nose toward the sky. The boys froze in their tracks. Afraid to take their eyes off of the dog.

"Don't look at its eyes, be careful."

"I can't help it. I looked in the dog's eyes."

"Say a prayer quickly. Maybe that will save your soul."

"Dear God, please don't let my soul go to hell."

In a split second the black dog was gone. No one heard it leave or noticed any movement. It was like it disappeared.

"Where did it go?"

"I don't care as long as it is gone."

"Let's get out of here," Cecil said as he grabbed his brother John's shirt tale.

"Which way are we going?" William asked.

"Anyway, you can."

"Papa, Papa, we saw the black dog. It had white eyes, just like you said. Cecil thinks he looked into its eyes. He said a prayer. Will that keep his soul from going to hell?"

"It's hard to say boys. You shouldn't have looked into its eyes."

"I couldn't help it. I was drawn to them."

"Well, boys, was the fright worth the promise of good luck?" Uncle Albert asked.

"I don't know if it was or not."

"What if we see the black dog for the second time? Sorrow will follow, and I don't like the thought of that."

"Me either," Cecil said.

"Me either," John said.

"Chances are you will see the black dog again," Papa told them.

"Why did you let us go look for the dog Papa?" John asked.

"Because there are somethings you have to learn on your own John. If your Uncle Albert and I told you not to go look for the black dog, then you would have wanted to go even more. You only thought about the promise of good luck and didn't consider the consequences of your actions. Let this be a lesson to you."

"We will Papa, we will."

Trixie Dog

1946

My Aunt and Uncle, Rhetha and Owen always lived on a farm. They had several dogs, cats and kittens, chickens and Jersey cows.

One summer a small yellow puppy showed up at their farm. Their other two dogs, Queen and Indy Girl accepted her, so they kept her and named her Trixie.

She was special from the start; sweet, smart, a good watch dog and kind to children. Trixie grew up to weigh thirty pounds and had a beautiful golden coat.

Uncle Owen said she was the best cow dog he ever had. In the late afternoon he sent Trixie to gather the cows from the field. She rounded them up and brought them to the barnyard for milking.

Uncle Owen swore she could count. If all of the cows weren't in the barnyard he would ask her, "Is that all of them?"

Trixie would look around the barnyard, then return to the field to bring in the cows that were still grazing.

My brother Joe loved Trixie and she loved him. They would run and play in the yard whenever he and my Mother visited. Joe was four years old at the time.

Queenie and Indy Girl had gotten old so they left the herding to Trixie.

One day when my Mother and Brother visited the farm my Mother noticed that Aunt Rhetha seemed sad.

"Is something the matter Rhetha?"

"We'll talk about it later."

"I'm going outside to play with Trixie," my brother said.

"Don't go out now. It's too hot. Why not play with your toy soldiers in the living room," Aunt Rhetha told Joe.

Joe went to play and the women went in the kitchen.

"So, what's wrong?"

"Yesterday, Trixie died after delivering three dead puppies. Owen buried her on the shady side of the barn. Let's wait until he gets home before we tell Joe about it."

"Oh, that's so sad! Joe's heart will be broken."

"I know it."

The women were busy fixing supper and didn't hear Uncle Owen's truck come in. As usual he parked his truck beside the shed and crossed through the barnyard.

Joe had heard the truck and went out the front door. Queenie and Indy Girl were sitting in the yard. Joe went around the house and walked out the gate into the barnyard just as Uncle Owen opened the big gate for the cows to come through.

Jersey cows are normally passive except when they are coming in for their sweet feed. Then it's almost like a stampede.

Uncle Owen opened the gate and the cattle ran into the barnyard. Uncle Owen turned and saw Joe standing directly in the path of the cows.

"Joe, hurry, get out of the way!"

Joe stood still. The women ran out of the house. When they saw what was happening, they screamed at Joe to run. He didn't move.

Five steps before running over Joe the cows parted in different directions. As if something had stopped them.

Uncle Owen grabbed Joe and took him to the yard.

"Joe, you could have been killed. Why didn't you move when we told you to?"

"Trixie dog was with me. I knew she wouldn't let the cattle hurt me."

"Joe, Trixie couldn't have been with you. We didn't want to tell you but she died yesterday."

"That can't be true. I saw her. After she stopped the cows, she ran back to the shady side of the barn."

"It must have been Queenie or Indy Girl."

"It was Trixie!"

"Owen, show Joe where you buried her."

Uncle Owen took Joe's hand and they started across the barnyard. When they reached the spot where Joe had been standing Uncle Owen saw paw prints all over the ground. They followed the paw prints. They led directly back to Trixie's grave."

Though it seemed impossible, they all came to believe that Trixie's spirit returned to earth to save Joe from being killed.

The Walking Table

1949

Not long after my Mama and Daddy got married, they would go to my Grandparents House on Saturday nights. Mama's sisters and brothers came too and they would play Rook or Chinese checkers.

My Uncle Cecil was a building contractor. While renovating an old home he found a Ouija board in the attic. On this Saturday night he brought the Ouija board with him figuring everyone would get a laugh out of it somehow. My Grandmother, Mom Henry didn't like it the second she saw it.

"I don't want that thing in my house," she protested, "take it outside or put it back in your car."

"Oh, come on Mom, it's just a silly game board, it's all in fun."

"It may be fun for you but it's not fun for me. Go on and get that thing out of my house."

"Yes, Ma'am," my uncle replied. He carried the Ouija board back to his car. An hour or so passed and Mom Henry was sitting on the front porch talking to her cousin Marguerite.

"Go get the Ouija board. Mom's talking to Marguerite, she'll never know it," my Aunt Lil told her brother.

"What do you all think?"

"Go get it. I'm tired of playing rook," my Daddy Hanly answered.

"I agree, go get it," my Mama Rosa said, then continued, "besides Papa has beaten me three straight checker games. Let's do something else."

Papa had gone into the front room to look at a new catalog that had come in the mail that day. He wasn't paying any attention to what was going on in the kitchen.

Cecil got the Ouija board from his car and brought it inside. He sat the board on the kitchen table and everyone took a seat. There seemed to be a sense of excitement in the air, or maybe it was a fear of the unknown.

"Who's going to ask the questions?" My Aunt asked.

"I don't want to ask the questions," Mama replied.

"I'll ask the questions, it's my Ouija board," Cecil told them.

"Fine with me," everyone said in agreement.

"Now put your finger right here on this triangle thing, like this."

My uncle placed his pointer finger on the triangle and the other's followed suit.

"Don't push the triangle with your finger. Just let it float around the board."

"The first question is. Is today Saturday?"

"What kind of question is that?" My Daddy asked.

"I want to start out with a simple question," Cecil replied.

"Now, everyone concentrate. Is today Saturday?" Cecil asked the Ouija board.

The triangle started to move across the board.

"Are you all pushing on it?"

"I'm not."

"Neither am I, I swear."

The triangle moved to the word yes.

"Wow, that was something. Ask it another question,"

"Will it rain tomorrow?'"

The triangle moved with ease to the other side of the board and stopped on the word no.

"Oh, that was creepy."

"Mom Henry came into the kitchen, "What is that thing doing on my kitchen table?" I told you to put it back in your car. Get it off my kitchen table right now. I've heard a Ouija board on a kitchen table will cause the food to spoil. Hurry now, get it off, and wash the table with salt and holy water. Then we will say a prayer over it."

"Yes, ma'am, yes, ma'am."

The board was folded away. The table was washed off with Mom Henry's recipe for removing evil and a prayer was said. Surely all would be right now.

Mom and Papa went on to bed early because they were tired. The others straightened up the house and went out and sat on the front porch.

"Go get the Ouija board again, I thought that was fun," Lil said to Cecil.

"We don't have a table out here on the front porch. You've got to have a table."

"We could use that one drawer table. You know, the one in the front room."

"I suppose we could at that. I'll get the board, you get the table."

My Daddy carried the table out of the house and sat it on the porch.

The board was sat up on the one drawer table and everyone resumed their positions.

"Will I be a rich man?" My uncle asked the board.

This time the triangle started toward the word yes, then turned toward no, and stopped in the middle of the board.

"I guess that means it doesn't know for sure."

They all got a big laugh from that.

The next question asked was, "What is our parents last name?"

The triangle moved to the letter H first.

"Are you pushing that thing?"

"No, we're not."

The triangle moved to the letter E next. And before they knew it, the board had spelled out N, R, Y.

"It spelled Henry, it spelled Henry!" Rosa proclaimed.

"I don't believe it. Somebody's pushing that thing around."

They all looked at each other.

"Ask a spooky question."

"Like what?"

"Ask if the Ouija board has the devil in it?"

"I don't like that question."

"Go on, ask it."

My Uncle moved around in his chair. He wiped his sweating hands on his pants. He cleared his throat and asked, "Ouija board, do you have the devil in you?"

In less than three seconds the pointer went to the word yes.

"That's enough for me."

"Me too, it's scary."

"Oh well," my uncle said, "I'll put it back in the car. Besides it's getting late, we all better be going home."

Daddy picked up the table and carried it back to the front room. Everyone went in the front door, and locked it behind them.

"I think I'll have another bite of the pecan pie. Get us some plates."

My Aunt sliced the pie as everyone sat down at the table. As they were eating the pie, they heard someone knocking at the front door.

"Wonder who that is?" Mama asked.

"I'll see who it is," Lil said, as she walked down the hall to the front door.

She returned to the kitchen and said, "There wasn't anyone there."

"Sure, sounded like someone knocking."

They heard the noise again.

"I'll see what it is this time," Daddy told them.

Instead of walking down the hall, he cut through the front room.

"Ouch," he said.

"What is it?" Mama asked him in a scared voice.

"I ran into the table."

"What table?"

"The one drawer table, I know I sat it back against the wall."

"I saw you put it against the wall," my Aunt replied.

"How did it get out there in the middle of the floor?" My uncle asked. Mama flipped on the front room light and spoke. "You must not have sat it against the wall."

"Yes, I did," Daddy answered.

"I saw him put it there," Lil added.

"That is strange, I'll put the table back in its place."

My Uncle picked up the table and sat it against the wall. He had barely turned around when the table started moving by itself.

"Oh, Lord, look at that!"

Mama and Lil screamed and retreated back into the kitchen. From there they watched as the table scooted across the floor.

My Grandparents came into the kitchen asking. "What in the world is going on?"

"We took the one drawer table out front and sat the Ouija board on it. Now the table is walking by itself."

"I told you to put that board back in your car. Now you've brought the devil back into my house!" Mom was visibly upset.

Papa stepped into the front room and saw the table in the middle of the room. The table started moving across the floor again.

"There's only one thing to do," he proclaimed.

"What Papa, what can we do?"

"Go get our bible, it's beside our bed. Go get it now."

Mama hurried to get the bible and returned to the kitchen with it.

"Here Papa," she handed him the bible.

Papa picked up the table and returned it to its place on the wall. He opened the drawer and put the bible in there. He motioned for the others to join him and reluctantly they did.

"We need to say the Lord's prayer together." Papa began the prayer and the others joined in.

My uncle burned the Ouija board the next day in his burn pile. The table never walked on its own again. But just in case, a bible has been kept in the drawer for the last seventy years to prevent the devil from returning.

Cave Hill Gentleman

1974

Cave Hill Cemetery is named for a large cave with an ever-flowing spring on site. Located in Louisville, Kentucky, it was established as a county cemetery in 1848. Encompassing more than fifty acres, it has the feel of a public park filled with indigenous trees and bushes of Kentucky. There are large mausoleums and elaborate tombstones throughout the cemetery. Several famous people are buried there, including Colonel Harlan Sanders. There were so many requests for directions to his grave that the cemetery committee painted yellow lines on the road leading to his grave.

A couple, Joe and Faye, were visiting Cave Hill Cemetery. It was a cool spring day and there weren't many visitors on the grounds.

While enjoying the solitude of the cemetery, Joe noticed a man standing on a nearby grave. He remembered thinking how hard it was to be by yourself anymore. With all the acreage in the cemetery, this man had to be right there with him.

He turned to look for his wife and saw her about a hundred feet away. He turned back and looked at the man standing on a grave. He described him as being in his sixties, around five feet ten inches tall, dark hair combed straight back, his face was very pale. He wore an outdated grey broadcloth suit with a white shirt and herringbone vest, and large heavy boots. The man stood there upon the grave, looking down.

Joe turned to look for his wife again and when he glanced back toward the man he was gone. Joe looked all around but didn't see him anywhere. He called to his wife.

"Faye, did you see that man over there?"

"No, I didn't see anyone."

Joe decided to explore. He walked to the grave and looked down. There on the soft spring ground of the grave were two large footprints. There weren't any footprints leading to or from the grave, just the two where Joe had seen the man standing.

The tombstone read:

William F. Richardson
Born December 16th, 1800,
Died March 15th, 1864,
A Confederate prisoner in Louisville, Kentucky.

The inscription on the tombstone read, "Greater than Lee, he didn't surrender."

A thought suddenly dawned on Joe. That day was March the 15th. It had been exactly one hundred and ten years since the man had died.

Joe didn't consider it a coincidence. He believed he had seen the spirit of William Richardson visiting his own grave on the anniversary of his death.

Made in the USA
Columbia, SC
06 March 2022

57118810R00109